Critical Theory &
African Literature Today
19

African Literature Today

Editor: Eldred Durosimi Jones
* 1, 2, 3, and 4 Omnibus Edition
5 The Novel in Africa
6 Poetry in Africa
7 Focus on Criticism
8 Drama in Africa
* 9 Africa, America & the Caribbean
*10 Retrospect & Prospect
11 Myth & History

Editor: Eldred Durosimi Jones
Associate Editor: Eustace Palmer
Assistant Editor: Marjorie Jones
12 New Writing, New Approaches
*13 Recent Trends in the Novel
*14 Insiders & Outsiders
1-14 were published from London by
Heinemann Educational Books and from
New York by Africana Publishing
Company

The new series is published by
James Currey Publishers and Africa World Press
*ALT 15 Women in African Literature Today
*ALT 16 Oral & Written Poetry in African Literature Today
*ALT 17 The Question of Language in African Literature Today
*ALT 18 Orature in African Literature Today
*ALT 19 Critical Theory & African Literature Today

*Copies of back issues marked with an asterisk may be purchased from your
bookseller or direct from James Currey Ltd

Future Issues

Place a standing order with your supplier for future issues

ALT 20 New Writers in African Literature
This issue will examine the works of writers who have appeared (or have
developed significantly) in the last two decades in any of the genres. (Articles now
being edited).

ALT 21 Childhood in African Literature
Childhood is a frequently recurring theme in African literature which runs
through all the genres – poetry, the novel, drama and autobiography. Camara
Laye's The African Child and Wole Soyinka's Aké have taken their place as
classics in this kind. Deadline for the submission of articles has passed.

ALT 22 Exile & African Literature
Articles are invited on the influence of exile on the literature of Africa and its
significance in the work of particular writers. Deadline for the submission of
articles June 1995.

Before embarking on articles contributors are advised to submit proposals to the
Editor, Professor Eldred Durosimi Jones: Fourah Bay College, University of Sierra
Leone, Private Mail Bag, Freetown, Sierra Leone. Unsolicited articles are wel-
come, but will not be returned unless adequate postage arrangements are made
by the contributors.

All articles should be well typed, double spaced on A4 paper with a wide margin.
References to books should include the author or editor, place, publisher, date and
the relevant pages.
Contributors must keep a spare copy in case of loss in transit.

Critical Theory & African Literature Today

A review
Editor: ELDRED DUROSIMI JONES
Associate Editor: EUSTACE PALMER
Assistant Editor: MARJORIE JONES

JAMES CURREY
LONDON

AFRICA WORLD PRESS
TRENTON N.J.

James Currey
an imprint of Boydell and Brewer Ltd,
PO Box 9, Woodbridge, Suffolk IP12 3DF, UK
and 668 Mount Hope Avenue, Rochester NY 14620-2731, USA
www.jamescurrey.com
www.boydell and brewer.com

Africa World Press, Inc.
PO Box 1892
Trenton
NJ 08607

A catalogue record is available from the British Library

ISBN 978–0–85255–519–4

p

Transferred to digital printing

Typeset in 10/12pt Melior Colset Pte. Ltd., Singapore

Contents

Editorial Article
Critics & Creators

Eldred D. Jones

The criticism of modern African literature has developed side by
side with the literature itself and though, interestingly, some of its
foremost critics are among its foremost creators, it cannot be said
that the latter, in Pope's phrase, turned critics merely in their own
defence. Theirs has been a genuine search for a poetic to accommodate a literature arising out of the African tradition expressed
largely in non-African languages and reflecting an environment
which in its mannerisms, its artefacts and even in its morality may
be far removed from its traditional roots. Indeed some of the finest
examples of African literary criticism are to be found in the works
of these same creative writers. The negritude poets, particularly
Senghor, Césaire and Damas, led the way with their theory and
practice in the Paris of the 1930s. Their work is examined here
by Isaac Elimimian.

Kofi Awoonor, whose criticism is discussed in Obi Maduakor's
article, sought inspiration for his practice from the traditional
poetry of the Ewe and his study particularly of the dirge form has
been a considerable influence on his writing, so that his poetry
though written in English is very close in spirit and in imagery to
the traditional Ewe dirge. In his criticism in turn he looks for a
similar Africanness in the literature and judges the success or
failure of a work from the point of view of its realisation of this
quality. In so far as Chinweizu et al.[1] sought an anchor for their
criticism of modern African literature in traditional practice, the
oral tradition, their starting point was not very different from that
of Kofi Awoonor. But in so far as their prescription was restric-
tive – and it remained so even when they had shifted away from
the insistence that African literature can only be written in

1

African languages – their prescription was far too limiting for a literature that would express the changing African environment. Wole Soyinka similarly undertakes an examination of tragedy with the Yoruba tragic ritual drama as his starting point,[2] Yoruba tragedy as it reflects the Yoruba world-view. But he is also very conscious that even in traditional Yoruba society this world-view itself is not static. Perhaps the most significant feature of his criticism of tragedy is that it situates the Yoruba tragic view in the wider context of human tragedy, so that Yoruba tragic drama is a manifestation of the puny human being, man, responding to the tremendous cosmic forces around him. Soyinka's excursions into the nature of tragedy take him beyond the Yoruba civilisation or the particular Yoruba predicament into the general human condition. As in his creative work he penetrates through to 'the common denominators of humanity'. The criticism thus embraces the fate of an Oba Koso as well as a Lear, as each struggles within himself for a reconciliation of conflicting cosmic forces. There is in Soyinka's creative and critical practice a consciousness of the universal element in human activity.

This concept of universality is angrily rejected in Achebe's criticism when for instance, in an essay in *Morning Yet on Creation Day*, he asks, 'Am I being told for Christ's sake that before I write about any problem I must first verify whether they have it too in New York and London and Paris?'[3] The answer is certainly, no. Universality concerns the degree to which a work penetrates to the essence of the human condition within its own context. Indeed, to be truly universal is to be truly local. The fact that such penetration may also strike chords elsewhere is incidental and in his best work in which he focuses attention on a particular Igbo or Nigerian situation and gets to the essential truth of it, Achebe's work displays this quality which may contribute to the possibility of universal acceptance but neither awaits it nor depends on it.

These critics all start their search for a poetic in the African oral tradition but this may not be the only route. The African critic like his creative counterpart comes to his work with the baggage (perhaps the impedimenta) with which his borrowed language and its civilisation have equipped or burdened him. J. P. Clark, the title of whose critical volume, *The Example of Shakespeare*, reveals one of the sources of his literary equipment, comes to critical judgement through an examination of Shakespeare's work. Examining the portrayals of Aaron, Othello and Caliban, he notes that Shakespeare avoids the option of giving these characters a sub-standard form of English. Instead, he distinguishes them from the other characters (and incidentally one from each other) by the particular kinds of imagery which he gives them. Clark applies Shakespeare's method to the portrayal of African characters by African authors using English:

> This is why the Shakespearean solution seems to me the supreme example for the African writer in a European language to follow . . . it should be possible to tell the Ibo farmer Okonkwo in Mr Achebe's *Things Fall Apart* from the Ijaw fisherman, Zifa, in my *Song of a Goat*: references of the one naturally incline more to barnyards and harvests as those of the other to fishlines and tides.[4]

Njabulo Ndebele, in *Rediscovery of the Ordinary*,[5] examines the products of a mainly urban South African tradition of writing which does not seem to be as much rooted in traditional African culture. While the African element is predominant in both the creative and critical stances of an Achebe or an Awoonor, the overwhelming and overriding cultural phenomenon in South African writing is apartheid. (A quite different tradition informs the oral literature with which, say, Daniel Kunene is concerned.) According to Ndebele's thesis, the culture of South Africa is the culture of spectacle manifested in everything from the blatant social divisions to the exhibitionism of its football. It is a culture whose main feature is its exteriority which is reflected in the literature. The mere cataloguing of the obvious surfaces of things, the self-evident inequities, have hitherto constituted a protest. This pre-occupation with protest condemns the literature to a propagandist role, and produces case-makers rather than story-tellers. The injection of irony would contribute to the production of an artistic tradition which is largely absent from the output of South African writers. What is required according to Ndebele, is a new vision, the transcendence of the protest posture. South African literature should rediscover the 'ordinary' which includes a concern with the rural environment and liberate itself from the mesmerising lure of the township. How far this search for the ordinary in the rural setting will lead back to the traditional roots in oral literature remains to be seen.

The South African situation is something of an exception in sub-Saharan Africa. In most other areas both the writer and the critic are caught up in a fast changing world where the traditional exists side by side with the (for want of a better word) 'modern' or urban. Even in this modern setting, however, there are survivals of the traditional in various degrees ranging from sometimes highly choreographed evocations of the traditional quite remote from commitment or belief, to simple ceremonies arising directly from personal conviction, not to mention more devilish, more cynical exploitations of the so-called tradition. The most abiding repositories of tradition in the urban setting are the African languages themselves which survive in competition with the acquired languages of Europe and they include the vigorous urban pidgins and creoles, whose literature is the subject of Ezenwa-Ohaeto's article. This contemporaneity may itself lead to ambiguities. But even the most urban setting in Africa is still African, and its inhabitants carry within themselves at least fading echoes of the tradition.

The poetics of African literature will change and the direction of change is likely to be further and further away from the outward mannerisms of the traditional culture just as modern urban life is moving further and further away. Soyinka's characters in *The Interpreters* manifest these ambiguities. Their allegiance to the Yoruba pantheon is artistic rather than religiously devout. The gods of tradition have become, for many urban Africans, metaphors rather than living forces whom they believe capable of influencing their lives except through the medium of art. The gods have lost their mystery. It is to the extent that writers are able to realise the vanishing influences of tradition in the modern situation – rather than tagging bits of 'traditionalia' on to their writings – that their works will represent the true modern African situation.

The danger with an African poetic which is rigidly married to traditional practice or a mummified traditional ethic is that it will not provide an adequate frame of reference for the production of significant literature or for the examination of it. It is possible, for example, to envisage an African novel, which has no obvious physical manifestations of traditional culture; set in a modern African city with characters who have been completely severed from pristine tradition. The urban South African novel may already point to this possibility. A poetic which limits an African work to one which participates in the outward manifestations of the traditional African culture will be an inadequate vehicle for the portrayal of the truth of African contemporary life.

African literature and its criticism exist in the context of other literatures and other schools of criticism. Literary theories developed in different literary environments are available and even insistently so, to African writers and their critics. Sunday Anozie's structuralist approach to the poetry of Christopher Okigbo was something of a surprise in 1972,[6] but Emmanuel Yewah in this issue puts forward a critical manifesto which embraces not only narratology (the subject of Leif Lorentzon's article) but even deconstruction; and clearly the starting point for Ify Achufusi's examination of the works of Flora Nwapa is a feminist criticism which developed outside Africa. Some of the most forthright pronouncements on the role of the writer and critic from the Marxist point of view are to be found in the writings of Ngũgĩ wa Thiong'o. His moral vision was rooted in the virtues of Kikuyu civilisation but he saw the task of the modern writer and critic as one which is to unite with a global socialist ideal: 'He must ... find his true creative links with the pan-African masses over the earth in alliance with all the socialistic forces of the world.'[7] Olu Obafemi's critical stance in this issue is also obviously influenced by Marxist critical theory. So long as such critical theories are not prescriptively applied they could be useful in the illucidation of African literature.

How does African literature stand in relation to critical theories which have either decreed, or in their criticism accomplished, the death of the author? The great gift to literary criticism of the so-called new critics (mainly American) of the 1940s and '50s was the rescue of literature from generalisations which paid insufficient attention to the text and often concerned itself with biographical irrelevancies. The new critics restored the centrality of text but did not quite accomplish the elimination of the author. In traditional African societies there is no ambiguity about the centrality of the author/presenter and from this tradition it is easy to derive Achebe's 'novelist as teacher'. Indeed the social responsibility of the writer has been stressed over and over by both creators and critics. In the words of Okello Oculi:

The exhausted starved labourer needs more from the creative writer than the cries of Romeo to the supposedly tender ears of Juliet. The mother whose children have been scorched by napalm bombs demands a cry against murder and war from the artist and not fantasies on the silence beyond tropical siestas.[8]

This teaching role is sufficiently high in the expectation of the consumer of African literature that African critics should not be too eager to join in this assault of the author. This and similar caveats may be necessary in the face of fashionable theories emanating from other traditions.

Every significant work of art projects a moral vision from the particular standpoint of its creator and through the particular stand from which he attempts to engage the sensibilities of the receiver. It is the business of the critic to respond fully to the work of art and communicate his response which should not be a mere application of critical theories but a total response to the moral vision.

Some thirty years ago, I came across a critic who, in a desperate effort to rescue literary criticism from the charge of being unscientific, of being a merely subjective response, attempted to devise what he called a slide rule for measuring the arts. This is probably the same sort of drive that leads to some of the more mechanical approaches to the study of literature. The critic's judgement is eventually subjective but his must be an educated and sensitive subjectivity, using all the tools at his disposal.

Christopher Okigbo's poetry is probably a better route to his critical perceptions than some of his provocative critical remarks which only cause misunderstanding. His search in *Heavensgate* was not an attempt to return to traditional Igbo life; it was the search of a modern African artist for a spiritual anchor in a modern materialist society using the full resources of his traditional background as well as his western education and experience, achieving in the result, a totally harmonised poetic form. His attainment of this spirituality may be merely momentary, fragmentary, coming in flashes, but how well does he realise this evanescent vision in the following passage whose full exposition will take us well into the depths of Igbo traditional beliefs:

Bright
with the armpit-dazzle of a lioness
she answers,

wearing white light about her;

and the waves escort her,
my lioness,
crowned with moonlight.

So brief her presence –
match-flare in wind's breath –
so brief with mirrors around me.

Downward . . .
the waves distil her:
gold crop
sinking ungathered.

Watermaid of the salt emptiness,
grown are the ears of the secret.[9]

The critic's attempts may be equally groping, inconclusive but occasionally enlightening.

NOTES

1. Chinweizu *et al.*, *Towards the Decolonisation of African Literature* (Enugu: Fourth Dimension, 1980).
2. Wole Soyinka, *Myth, Literature and the African World* (Cambridge: Cambridge University Press, 1976).
3. Chinua Achebe, *Morning Yet on Creation Day* (London: Heinemann, AWS, 1975) 50.
4. J. P. Clark, *The Example of Shakespeare* (London: Longman, 1970) 23.
5. Njabulo S. Ndebele, *Rediscovery of the Ordinary* (Johannesburg: COSAW, 1991).
6. Sunday O. Anozie, *Christopher Okigbo: Creative Rhetoric* (London: Evans, 1972, African Writers and their Work).
7. Ngũgĩ wa Thiong'o, *Writers in Politics: Essays* (London: Heinemann Educational Books, 1981) 79–80.
8. Andrew Gurr and Angus Calder, *Writers in East Africa* (Nairobi: East African Literature Bureau, 1974) 28.
9. Christopher Okigbo, *Heavensgate* (Ibadan: Mbari Publications, 1962) 25.

Obi Maduakor

The Ghanaian poet Kofi Awoonor, a major voice in Ghana's literary scene, has been engaged in creative activity since the publication by Mbari of his first book of verse, *Rediscovery* in 1964. A contemporary of the Nigerian poet, Christopher Okigbo, he sees himself as one of the creators of the style and technique of modern African poetry.[1] He belongs to the first generation of modern African writers. Awoonor has published five books of poetry, two novels, and a selection of Ewe oral poetry which he edited.[2] He has also distinguished himself as a critic and it is his achievement in this genre that this essay attempts to evaluate.

In 1975 Awoonor published *The Breast of the Earth; a survey of the history, culture and literature of Africa south of the Sahara.* He has in addition published some essays in literary journals, and has granted several interviews to scholars, in which he expressed his views about his own writing and the work of other African writers.

Awoonor is a keen student of oral literature. His critical interests rest in the domain of poetry, both oral and written, and in the relationship between the two. *The Breast of the Earth* is, in fact, a revised and enlarged version of his doctoral thesis submitted in 1973 to State University of New York at Stony Brook under the title 'The Influences of Oral Literature on Contemporary Literature of Africa'. The major part of his criticism of African works is contained in the revised and published version of this study.

But there is an essay that is seminal, and the background to that essay is helpful in understanding Awoonor's position both as a critic and as a writer. In 1973 the Nigerian critic, Michael Echeruo, unaware of the network of interlinking motifs unifying the various elements in Awoonor's first novel *This Earth, My Brother* (1971) dismissed it hastily as incoherent since it lacks the mediating presence of a central intelligence who would interpret the experiences in the novel for the reader.[3] Earlier on in 1971, Charles Larson published his book *The Emergence of African Fiction* written from a magisterial standpoint, with the author pontificating on what is or is not African literature. These critical responses first to his work and secondly to African writing in general compelled Awoonor to formulate what amounts to, for him, aesthetic modalities for the critical judgement of African literature. The propositions are articulated in the seminar paper 'Tradition and Continuity in African Literature', which he delivered to the students and African Studies faculty of the University of Washington in 1973. At this seminar Awoonor said: 'No critical approach to African writing in English, French, or Portuguese can ignore the aesthetics, concepts of time, ontological systems and perceptions of the world which most of the writers bring to their work. It is from this that the literature will have to be judged.'[4] Awoonor proceeds in that talk, but with greater clarity and emphasis in the version of it published later in *Exile and Tradition*, to articulate the features of the African world-view and its aesthetics. He comes up with four propositions which are as follows:

(a) The traditional artist is both a technician and a visionary. As a technician he excels in the management of his material: words, wood, stone, raffia, etc; and as a visionary he inscribes his work simultaneously within the visible world and the invisible world of essence and spirituality.

(b) The artistic process is a process of transformation which entails a primary exchange of energies through what might be called the magical projection. In this projection everything is possible and permissible and miracles happen.

(c) The artistic process encloses a self-generating ecstasy or moments of delirious madness, the breaking down of the formalities of the perceived reality. But the poet overcomes these crises sustained by his willpower, which enables him to impose order upon chaos. Poetry, dance, carving, represent in their finished states the serenity which is the enduring aspect of the resolved crisis of the artist's divine person.

(d) African art aspires ultimately towards the condition of wholeness. It aims at evoking energies that make for restoration,
renewal and integration; it does not provoke disintegration either
within the individual or the communal psyche.[5]

This last point is conceived clearly with Awoonor's own work in
mind. The termination of Amamu's quest, the hero of *This Earth,
My Brother*, in madness, has puzzled many a critic. But Awoonor
insists that the contradictions within his hero's psyche are
resolved at that moment of his final embrace with the woman of
the sea. It is at that moment that he, like Joyce's hero whom he
so consciously recalls, attains a state of aesthetic grace.[6]

Awoonor claims that the above formulation is the traditional
aesthetics within which he operates as a writer. Other writers
that work in the same tradition are Amos Tutuola, Wole Soyinka
(consciously echoed in the formulation of the aesthetics themselves), and Chinua Achebe. It might be necessary before returning to *The Breast of the Earth* to consider briefly how the above
theory can be illustrated with the work of the writers sharing the
same kindred spirit with Awoonor. Tutuola's case is illustrated
amply in *The Breast of the Earth* where the tales are shown to
represent a quest thematically conforming to the structure of
the heroic monomyth, consisting of departure, initiation and
return. The hero's initiation would correspond to the crisis of
artistic creation, and the return to the wholeness that leads to
re-integration and restoration.

In Soyinka's novel, *The Interpreters*, each of the major characters, Sagoe, Egbo, Bandele, Sekoni, Kola, is an interpreter, that is,
an artist seeking to infuse a moral balance into a fast disinte-
grating world. Kola carries in his person the urgent energy of the
artist as he seeks to create on his great canvas the re-assembled
folk psyche, peopled by deities and men in a unified community.
But it is Bandele, the Obatala essence, who restores through the
serenity of his person all the fragmented energies of his friends
and of the world to a state of calm which is a precondition and
prelude to the progression and the expansion of the human
circle.

In Achebe's first novel, things did not fall apart, the centre held,
for it was only Okonkwo who decided to commit suicide. Umuofia
refused to commit suicide. In *Arrow of God* Ezeulu mistook his

vengeful will for the will of his god and is struck mad. His refusal to eat the yam spelt hardship for his community but his people rejected disaster and brought home the harvest in the name of his son. The victory is not for Christianity but for Umuaro.[7]

Awoonor argues his thesis with passion and conviction through the works he has selected to prove it; but we might run into trouble if we apply it wholesale to every species of African writing. How does the work of his kinsman, Ayi Kwei Armah, to come nearer home, fit into his proposition? Definitely there is no wholeness at the end of *The Beautyful Ones are Not Yet Born* or *Fragments*. Awoonor is to state later that writers like Yambo Ouologuem and Ayi Kwei Armah epitomise an era of intense despair aggravated by their status as writers in exile. That is to say that as exiles these writers might not really have grasped the essence of the African world-view, which puts into question Awoonor's own works written almost entirely in exile.

Always a sensitive and frank critic of his own works, Awoonor states that his novel, *This Earth, My Brother*, persistently misread by critics, is inspired by motifs from Ewe ontology. It is not concerned with the politics of the Nkrumah era but rather with a total ongoing historical process of fragmentation and decay. Amamu is the archetypal hero, priest and carrier who bears the burden of fragmentation and decay but achieves restoration, as already observed, for his community in that final encounter with the woman of the sea who represents Mother Earth, Mother Africa.

In 'Tradition and Continuity in African Literature' Awoonor concentrates on the aesthetics of oral literature. In his book *The Breast of the Earth* he delineates further features of the African world-view while expanding some aspects of its aesthetics. These are articulated as follows:

(a) Time is cyclical, uniting the living, the dead, and the yet unborn into one continuum. In his second novel, *Comes the Voyager at Last* (1992) Awoonor states that real time is not the mechanical time (clock time) that limits and destroys time's autonomy, but the mythic time which transforms all with its mystery and magic.[8]

(b) The ancestors attain the status of minor deities in death and are bound to the living by 'blood', which is the most dynamic force for the living. The ceremony of invocation, or libation, brings the dead, the living and the unborn together in a communion. (c) Art embodies a context that is spiritual since it is very often used in ritual and worship. Artistic creations are statements of man's homage to the gods; their makers form part of a communal spirituality, and are clean and unblemished during the period they were engaged in creating such objects. The function of the artist is close to that of the priest and at times he is one and the same person.[9]

Of all the traditional art forms, says Awoonor, the 'word' has the final authority. It is sacred and imbued with magical power. Its sacredness is proven by the efficacy of incantations and the solemnity of oath-taking. The poet who utters the word is endowed with great responsibility. He is the medium through which the god transmits his will. In Ewe ontology he receives his inspiration from the god of song (*hadzivodu*), and must pour libations and offer prayers to his god before he appears in public to perform.[10] We might conclude this overview of the African world-view and its aesthetics with Awoonor's own testimony of the impact of the word on his imagination:

> The magical and mysterious relationships defining only the very simple and the mundane have, beyond time and place, their anchorage in *words*. Our people say the mouth that eats salt cannot utter falsehood. For the mouth is the source of sacred words, of oaths, promises, prayer and assertions of our *being*, presence, affirmation. This is the source of my poetry, the origin of my commitment – the magic of the word in the true poetic sense.[11]

Awoonor goes on to discuss the stylistic devices of samples of traditional poetry in order to demonstrate how these forms have influenced the stylistic development of modern African poetry. Attention is focused on the elegy or the dirge form as the form that has affected most profoundly the imagination of the modern poet, for his muse is persistently tragic. Some of the poets who have adopted the dirge form are Mazisi Kunene, Awoonor himself, and Christopher Okigbo.

Kunene's poetry, though written, flows directly from the Zulu oral poetic tradition as he himself has often insisted. The conventions of the Zulu dirge do not differ remarkably from those of the Ewe dirge. There is the elegiac tone evoked by a string of

apostrophised addresses to the dead, which later gives way to a
tone of desolation expressed by various strategies, and of gentle
rebuke to the ancestors for permitting the tragedy; a rhythm
marked by a gentle tempo; an imagery derived from nature and
extended into the features of human personality, and vice versa,
intimating man's intimacy with nature; and the use of parallelisms
fostered by the technique of repetition. Awoonor offers a fine
critique of Kunene's poem 'Elegy', analysing its features. It is a
long poem and the opening lines reproduced here will give us a
feel of the work:

O Mzingeli Son of the illustrious clans
You whose beauty spreads across the Tukela estuary
Your memory haunts like two eagles
We have come to mourn the bleeding sun
We are the children of Ndungunya of the Dlamini clan.[12]

Okigbo began with the European tradition only to find his true
voice when he returned to the traditional dirge form in the poems
of *Path of Thunder*, his last testament. 'Elegy for Slip-Drums' owes
its impact almost entirely to the use of traditional idiom and motif,
employing the devices of repetition, proverbs, allusions and exten-
sive animal imagery borrowed entirely from the Igbo world. In
'Elegy for Alto' he offers himself willingly as a sacrificial ram, as
the ritual carrier to be slaughtered for the regeneration of a
blighted community:

O mother Earth, unbind me; let this be my testament;
Earth, unbind me; let me be the prodigal; let this be the ram's ultimate
prayer to the tether.[13]

As regards his own development Awoonor acknowledges his
indebtedness to the Ewe dirge as developed by the veteran bard
Vinoko Hesino Akpalu. Akpalu's dirge opens with a statement
about the mourner's condition, then moves into a general lamentation, and ends with a message, supplication or prayer to those that
have gone before (the ancestors). It again employs the devices of
repetition, parallelism, symbolism and allusion, and derives the
imagery from nature. Akpalu who lived to be 90 was a very
unhappy man, immensely lonely, for he was childless. His dirge
is a lament about his personal predicament. He often addresses
himself by name in his poems.

The Ewe dirge captivated Awoonor's imagination early as a poetic form. He is fascinated by its use of elegiac tone, direct statement, exhortation, and prayer. Here is Awoonor himself:

> Some of my earliest poetry was an attempt to take over from the dirge a series of segments or individual lines around which to create longer pieces that still express a close thematic and structural affinity with the original.[14]

One of his poems born of this experiment, he says, is the beautiful poem 'Songs of Sorrow' whose opening lines read:

> Dzogbese Lisa has treated me thus
> It has led me among the sharps of the forest
> Returning is not possible
> And going forward is a great difficulty
> The affairs of this world are like the chameleon faeces
> Into which I have stepped
> When I clean it cannot go
> I am on the world's extreme corner,
> I am not sitting in the row with the eminent
> But those who are lucky
> Sit in the middle and forget
> I am on the world's extreme corner
> I can only go beyond and forget.[15]

The repetitions in this poem, the personalised sense of loss, and the mood of utter desolation are conventions borrowed from Akpalu. Farther down the line one can observe the dramatic voice of address ('My people, I have been somewhere') and other echoes from Akpalu. 'To be at the world's extreme corner' connotes a state of utter hopelessness such that the protagonist yearns for release in death. Awoonor analyses several of his poems modelled on the Ewe dirge, such as 'A Dirge' and the popular anthology piece 'I Heard a Bird Cry'. What he has taken from the Ewe dirge is its direct yet allusive style, its theme of sorrow, and its tone of lament.

Although Awoonor is critical of Negritude as a philosophical movement, he appreciates the poetry that is born of that movement. Negritude poetry enacts the gestures of traditional poetry. Its surrealistic mood, its fine manipulation of sound, rhythm, and the music of language share an affinity with Awoonor's own poetry. It celebrates the mystery of language and symbolism. It

achieves a unity of being through the evocation of smell, sugges-
tion of movement and gesture, form, texture and the total life-
force of African mythic landscape. In Aimé Césaire's *Cahier d'un
rétour au pays natal*, nature is the informing source of a poetry
embedded in mythical imagery and symbolism, and energised by
a sturdily delirious rhythm reminiscent of the ritual celebration
at sacred groves, and a unified sensibility that derives from a
trance-like surrealistic style.

Senghor celebrates the magical potency of his animal totems
and evokes a mythical landscape peopled by the dead ancestors,
memories of childhood and the presence of the mother who
becomes Mother Africa and the symbol of Black Immanence.
Alongside the woman, the dead and the ancestor, Senghor invokes
the ancestral masks which represent the visible symbolic link
between the living and the dead. David Diop also reveals an
instinctive attachment to the mystical motherhood where magic
and blood re-affirm for him, in exile, the spiritual bond with
ancestral earth. Dance functions for him as a symbol of the primal
life and of his dream Africa. He seeks to assert his unity with his
origin through a sensuous reclamation of the primary functions
of life symbolised by the magic of the dance and the achievement
of a state of trance, the harmony of sound, and the music of
language.

Poetry is the primary focus of Awoonor's interest in *The Breast
of the Earth*, and as a poet he does betray an unusual insight in
his analysis of oral and contemporary poetry. He also discusses
some works of fiction to balance out the book's perspective but the
writers selected are those manifestly influenced by a contact with
the African past, such as Tutuola and Achebe. Ngũgĩ and Oyono
are discussed as writers of the anti-colonial novel.

The essay on Tutuola is prefaced with the following preliminary
statement: 'In Tutuola's world, man and spirit exist in a unified
cosmic territory; the physical and the metaphysical coexist. Magic
and ritual are instruments of harmonizing those forces that may
be opposed to the weak nature of men who remain firmly at the
centre of this cosmic order.'[16] The main burden of the essay is to
demonstrate, as mentioned earlier, that Tutuola's tales enact the
paradigm of the heroic monomyth consisting of three archetypes:
departure, initiation, and return, the return being accompanied by
the hero's acquisition of an instrument of empowerment which he

deploys for the benefit of his community. The essay concludes with an equally remarkable observation:

> Tutuola's achievement rests in his going into the roots of Yoruba folk-lore to rediscover the great common soil of literature. This common soil yields nothing within the range of scientificalness or realism, but bases itself in magic, fantasy, mystery and the blatantly monstrous, expressing the most bizarre and incredible as the commonplace creations of Man's imagination.[17]

There is a veiled commendation of his own creative practice in between the lines of this eulogy. He too has gone back to the roots of his own folklore to 'uncover' materials out of which great literature is written. Because there is no absolute verisimilitude in his ordering of his fictional materials, he subtitles his stories 'tales'. They are not to be judged strictly in realistic terms, he says, but rather as an allegorical tale of an archetypal hero who journeys into himself and into the entrails of his society.[18]

Two of Achebe's novels offer interesting instances from the ontological point of view, the real perspective that engages Awoonor's critical interest in African novels. *Things Fall Apart* is hailed for being the first African novel to be wholly devoted to a significant African philosophical principle as a chief determinant of its construction. This principle is the concept of 'chi'. The theme of a man alone, dogged by jealous fate and abaited by unreliable gods is the concept around which every other image in the novel centres, the persistent image being that of the wrestler. Okonkwo is a man wrestling with his chi. He recalls in this role the little bird, 'nza', who challenged his chi to a contest after a heavy meal and lost.

The conflict in *Arrow of God* is rooted in the ontological concept of the priest and his proper perception of his mediatory role as the intermediary between man and the gods. In this role the priest is not only the carrier of the gods' truth but also the bearer of the sins of the people. He undergoes purification and cleansing in order to avert disaster. But Ezeulu is guilty of hubris which has led him to neglect his priestly office to his detriment. In a reading of his first novel, Awoonor insists on the destiny of his hero as a priest (he is 'a contemporary Ezeulu'[19]) and on the need for him to fulfil his duties as one, which naturally leads to self-immolation.

Apart from the exegesis on the symbolism of the Earth at the beginning of his chapter on Ngũgĩ wa Thiong'o in *The Breast of The Earth*, the two essays on Ngũgĩ and Oyono pursued in the spirit of straight criticism appear as uneasy bedfellows alongside the highly mythicised readings of Tutuola and Achebe. The disquisition on Earth symbolism is significant as it illuminates Awoonor's emotional fixation for Mother Earth which, one suspects, may have some connection with the matriarchal orientation of the Ewe society. Two of his works are 'named' (if one can put it that way) after Mother Earth, and his poetry alludes frequently to her. The Earth Goddess is the mother of all, a benevolent spirit upon whom man depends for food and sustenance, and to whom he returns at death. Earth is the place where man's umbilical cord is buried, and his link stretches through her to his ancestors who were buried in her womb.[20]

The Breast of the Earth is an ambitious work. Its scope is vast, embracing the history, culture, art and literature of black Africa. The best parts of the book are the literary sections which lie easily within Awoonor's competence. Gerald Moore[21] observes rightly that the book attempted far more than Awoonor would have been able to handle with confidence. The book is not altogether bereft of occasional 'dissertational garrulity' as certain points are over-belaboured for emphasis.

Awoonor has several essays tucked away in literary journals and magazines. Two will be discussed here: 'The Poem, the Poet, and the Human Condition', and 'The Imagery of Fire: A Critical Assessment of the Poetry of Joe de Graft'.[22] The first is partly a reaction to the Chinweizu school's naive conception of poetry, and partly a review of the work of some young Nigerian and Ghanaian poets. Its significance lies in the light it has thrown on Awoonor's insider-view of how the poet does his work. Reacting to the view of the Chinweizu school that poetry should be simple, Awoonor states that their insistence on the virtues of simplicity alone betrays a failure to come to terms with the creative process which is an embodiment of two basic dimensions, the accessible and the esoteric. Poetry operates at these two levels. The accessible exists in what in the poem is common property: the words, the sounds, the utterances, the public linguistic gestures and mannerisms of the poem. This aspect of the poem Awoonor calls 'the public market place' of the poem or its 'publicly owned linguistic landscape'.[23] Beyond this level is the real poem, the esoteric level where dwells the private man in the poem. It is the poem's hidden world, which is magical, enigmatic, existential and psychic. It is the element that explores and states the poem's ultimate private vision. The esoteric level of the poem conveys a meaning which does not correspond with information or facts. While the accessible level states the public domain of experience, the esoteric level leads 'into the inner shrine of the poet's self where the first man of the earth is met, raw, energetic, subtle and tragic in the full and complete splendour of his primal nakedness'.[24] In the true poem, such as the work of Ewe dirge poets, these two levels are unified.

The distinctions that Awoonor is labouring to establish here may not be different from Carl Jung's classification of the creative process into two modes: the psychological mode which is conscious and the visionary mode which is 'animystic'.[25] Whatever it is, Awoonor is at pains to pin it down with language. Hence there is a continuous search for definition. The most one can do is to guess that the accessible level is the poem's public world and the esoteric its mythical world.

In the second essay, Awoonor reviews the poetry of Joe de Graft, commending his work in his mature phase for the qualities we admire in his own poetry, namely, the insistent tone and energy of de Graft's poetry which reveals both technical competence and a great deal of introspective commentary on the affairs of men; and his ability to achieve a 'dramatic force within a series of open statements through the use of an internal dialogue, irony, sarcasm, and a tone of petulance bordering on anger'.[26] These qualities Awoonor has characterised as the 'imagery of fire'.

In an interview granted to Bernth Lindfors *et al.*, Awoonor responded to the crucial question of art and social/ideological commitment. The artist by the nature of the very commitment he imposes upon himself to tell the story of our woes, sorrows and joy is a committed writer, but on the ideological issue Awoonor is not so forthright in coming up with an answer. What he himself does as a writer is to let his own poetic truth engage historical truth in an after-dinner dialogue as it were. To make poetic truth precede history would be tantamount to pandering to ideological programming which would be bad art. Literature cannot be art and propaganda at the same time.[27] In the seminar version of 'Tradition and Continuity in African Literature' he delivered an aside on 'pseudo-revolutionary intellectuals of the Third World whose text is Fanon and who invest blood with a wondrous mystique'.[28] On the writer and his art, Awoonor states that a basic aestheticism inheres in every work of art (art is by its very nature beautiful). The aesthetic aspect can be perfected through an awareness of form which comes through studious application. What kind of critic is Awoonor? An urbane critic with mythic disposition. Being himself a myth-orientated writer whose work is difficult because it is frequently inscribed within the mythic consciousness, his criticisms are addressed to the issues of explicating his own works. In doing this he appeals to the aesthetics of the African world-view as paradigms through which his celebration of his own rites of passage can be appreciated.

NOTES

1. Bernth Lindfors *et al.*, eds, *Palaver: Interviews with Five African Writers* (Occasional Publications in African Literature, 3) (Texas: University of Texas Press, 1972) 51.
2. See appendix for publications by Kofi Awoonor.
3. 'Interview with Michael J. C. Echeruo', in *DEM-SAY: Interviews with Eight Nigerian Writers* (Occasional Publications in African Literature, 9) ed. Bernth Lindfors (Texas: University of Texas Press, 1974) 14.
4. Kofi Awoonor, 'Tradition and Continuity in African Literature', in *In Person: Achebe, Awoonor, and Soyinka*, ed. Karen L. Morell (Seattle: Institute for Comparative and Foreign Area Studies, 1975) 140.
5. Kofi Awoonor, 'Tradition and Continuity in African Literature', in *Exile and Tradition*, ed. Rowland Smith (London and Dalhousie: Longman and Dalhousie University Press, 1976) 167–70.
6. 'Interview with Kofi Awoonor' in *Talking with African Writers*, ed. Jane Wilkinson (London: James Currey, 1992) 28.
7. 'Tradition and Continuity in African Literature', *Exile and Tradition*, 166–72.
8. Kofi Awoonor, *Comes the Voyager at Last* (Trenton: Africa World Press, 1992) 102.
9. Kofi Awoonor, *The Breast of the Earth* (New York: NOK Publishers International, 1975) 50, 53 and 55.
10. Awoonor, 61, 65 and 115.
11. Kofi Awoonor, *Until the Morning After: Collected Poems 1963–1985* (New York: Greenfield Review Press, 1987) 216.
12. Awoonor, *The Breast of the Earth*, 194.
13. Awoonor, 224.

14. Awoonor, 202.
15. Awoonor, 203.
16. Awoonor, 227.
17. Awoonor, 250.
18. 'Interview with Kofi Awoonor', *Palaver*, 60.
19. 'Interview with Kofi Awoonor', *Talking with African Writers*, 28.
20. Awoonor, *The Breast of the Earth*, 283.
21. Gerald Moore, *Twelve African Writers* (London: Hutchinson, 1980) 260.
22. Kofi Awoonor, 'The Poem, the Poet and the Human Condition', *Asemka*, 5 (September 1979) 1-23; and Kofi Awoonor, 'The Imagery of Fire: A Critical Assessment of the Poetry of Joe de Graft', *Okike*, 19 (1981) 70-79.
23. Awoonor, 'The Poem, the Poet and the Human Condition', 21.
24. Awoonor, 20.
25. Carl Jung, 'Psychology and Literature', in *Modern Man in Search of a Soul* (London: Routledge and Kegan Paul, 1933) 177-83.
26. Awoonor, 'The Imagery of Fire', 76.
27. 'Interview with Kofi Awoonor', *Palaver*, 57.
28. 'Tradition and Continuity in African Literature', *In Person: Achebe, Awoonor and Soyinka*, 136.

Kofi Awoonor:
A Select Bibliography

Poetry

(George Awoonor-Williams) *Rediscovery and Other Poems* (Ibadan: Mbari, 1964).
Night of My Blood (New York: Doubleday, 1971).
Ride Me, Memory (Greenfield Center, NY: Greenfield Review Press, 1973).
The House by the Sea (Greenfield Center, NY: Greenfield Review Press, 1978).
Until the Morning After, Collected Poems 1963–1985 (Greenfield Center, NY: Greenfield Review Press, 1987, and Accra: Woeli Publishing Services, 1987). (Contains all Awoonor's previous collections, together with nine 'New Poems' and an autobiographical note).
Latin American and Caribbean Notebook (Trenton: Africa World Press, 1993).

Novels

This Earth, My Brother (New York: Doubleday, 1971).
Comes the Voyager at Last (Trenton: Africa World Press, 1992, and a new edition, Accra: Woeli Publishing Services, forthcoming).

Theatre

'Ancestral Power' and 'Lament' in *Short African Plays* (London: Heinemann, 1972) 1–11 and 119–28.

Criticism, Essays in History & Politics

The Breast of the Earth; a survey of the history, culture and literature of Africa south of the Sahara (New York: Doubleday, 1975).
The Ghana Revolution (New York: Oases, 1984).
Ghana: A Political History (Accra: Woeli Publishing Services and Sedco, 1990).

21

Negritude & African Poetry

Isaac I. Elimimian

The word, 'Negritude', which connotes 'blackness', has been employed in literary discourse for decades. Charles Lamb used the word in 1822 in his essay, 'The Praise of Chimney-Sweepers'.[1] Aimé Césaire employed it in 1938 in his poem *Return to my Native Land*: 'my negritude is not a stone/nor deafness flung out against the clamour of the day'.[2] In African literary criticism, Eldred Jones avers that Soyinka has little or no basis for attacking the Negritude writers since 'his work exhibits all that negritude was essentially about, bar the shouting'.[3]

My objective in this article is not only to highlight the use or the emergence of the word Negritude in literary criticism, but to discuss, as much as time and space permit, the theoretical background of the Negritude movement and its impact on African poetry, particularly as it applies to the works of Léopold Sédar Senghor, David Diop, and Birago Diop, Africa's best known Negritude poets.

Negritude, as a literary and cultural movement, was founded in the thirties by three black intellectuals: Léopold Sédar Senghor from Senegal, Aimé Césaire from Martinique, and Leon Damas from French Guyana. The fundamental objective of the movement and its founders was the need to define black aesthetics and black consciousness against a background of racial injustice and discrimination around the world.

Several external and internal factors contributed in various ways to the rise and development of the Negritude movement. With the abolition of the slave trade some individuals felt the need to explore avenues through which the unique contributions of the black man could be better documented or appreciated. For

22

instance, in 1897 Alexander Crummel founded the American Negro Academy whose mission was to promote black cultural values. In 1900, Sylvester Williams, a Trinidadian lawyer, collaborated with Bishop Alexander Walters of the African Episcopal Zion Church to organise in London the first pan-African Congress. And in 1910, W. E. B. Du Bois, in response to Booker T. Washington's writings and other activities, founded the National Association for the Advancement of Colored People (NAACP). There were also during this period the 'Back to Africa Movement' led by Marcus Garvey, as well as the surrealist movement inspired by André Breton which accorded pride of place to 'primitive' culture and civilisation. The desire to promote black consciousness and African cultural heritage was fuelled by the spate of discrimination and other injustices unleashed on the black man after the First World War and symbolised, for example, in the Italian invasion of Ethiopia in 1935.

Of the internal factors that inspired the rise of the Negritude movement, one can cite the following: the French policy of assimilation which attempted to propagate French civilisation at the expense of the indigenous culture; the discriminatory policies of French education to which people of African descent, particularly Aimé Césaire, Leon Damas, and Senghor, were subjected in France; and the fact that all three intellectuals were witnesses to the inadequacies of the Western civilisation which not only championed the philosophy that Africa had no history, no culture, but maintained that its people were created to be permanent hewers of wood and drawers of water. Aimé Césaire is credited with having first coined the word 'negritude' among the trio.

In African literature the critical debate regarding the objective and mission of the Negritude movement, as a worthwhile aesthetic endeavour, has raged on for decades. For instance while the francophone writers have generally emphasised the significance of Negritude as a major literary development, the anglophone authors, on the other hand, have generally dismissed it as irrelevant. Of the anglophone authors who have had a negative view of Negritude, one can cite the examples of Ezekiel Mphahlele, Christopher Okigbo, and Wole Soyinka. Mphahlele believed that the Negritude agenda was too romantic; Okigbo not only disliked the Negritude movement, but even turned down the 1966 Dakar Negro Festival of Arts Prize partly because he felt it developed from the Negritude concept which emphasised 'color'; while Soyinka, who coined the phrase 'a tiger does not proclaim its tigritude', thought that Negritude was based on too much noise rather than action.

The francophone African authors who have been Negritude's chief advocates – especially as demonstrated in their works – are Léopold Sédar Senghor, David Diop and Birago Diop, all three being poets and from Senegal. But why were these writers from the same country so deeply affected by the Negritude ethos on the continent? Gerald Moore and Ulli Beier offer the following explanation:

> Senegal is the only part of the African mainland which really witnessed *assimilation* in practice. Elsewhere it was not even attempted until after 1946 and was abandoned altogether as official policy some ten years later.[4]

Apart from having the same ancestral origin and going through the same assimilationist educational mill, all three men were motivated by their love of the fatherland and the ideals which inspired Negritude's orientation in the first place. It is for these reasons, perhaps more than anything else, that one finds in their work a complete glorification of Africa's cultural values.

Having discussed the genesis of the Negritude movement, the intellectual debate it has stimulated in African literature and the general impact it has had on Senghor, David Diop and Birago Diop, we shall now examine in more detail the way in which these poets have employed the Negritude philosophy to advance their poetry.

Léopold Sédar Senghor is undoubtedly the most prominent of the three. Born in 1906 in Joal, Senegal, of Christian parents, he was educated at the famous *Lycée* in Dakar and later at the Sorbonne in France. A man of many parts, poet, philosopher, critic, statesman – the first Senegalese indigenous president – he has to his credit several works through which he articulates his philosophy of Negritude. These include *Chants d'ombre* (1945), *Ethiopiques* (1956), *Hosties noires* (1958), and *Nocturnes* (1961).

Senghor defines Negritude as 'the awareness, defence, and development of African cultural values'.[5] It is this principle that underlies much of his poetry. But beyond this general principle, one can easily identify certain specific characteristics which distinguish his verse. For example, Senghor invokes and celebrates the dead ancestors, and he believes in the concept of the unity between the physical and the spiritual, that is, the dead and the living working together for the ultimate good of mankind. He also celebrates black beauty and African womanhood. And he believes that the ideals of both Western civilisation and African culture can and should be promoted for the benefit of the human race.

There are, of course, some critics who attack Senghor's Negritude for what they consider to be the inadequacies of its credo. Others believe that Negritude is patently discriminatory and thus itself falls a victim of racism by celebrating African culture at the expense of other civilisations. And there are those who heavily chide Senghor because they believe he has betrayed the Negritude cause by divorcing his African wife and marrying a white woman.

A theme which features prominently in Senghor's poetry is the celebration of the dead ancestors. In his treatment of this theme he reveals many things about traditional African culture, for example, that the dead ancestors are revered by the living for their ability to ward off evil or offer protection to the living; that in any human endeavour, little or nothing can be achieved without the active support and cooperation of the dead ancestors. Consequently, either in action or mood or feeling the dead are usually solicited – and sometimes prayers and sacrifices offered to them – especially in situations of need and danger.

In the poem 'In Memoriam', Senghor, apparently feeling lonely and insecure in Paris, the poem's setting, makes a fervent supplication to the dead ancestors:

Ah, dead ones who have always refused to die,
  who have known how to fight death
By Seine or Sine, and in my fragile veins
  pushed the invincible blood,
Protect my dreams as you have made your sons,
  wanderers on delicate feet. (p. 47)

Here in the above lines, another important belief is suggested about traditional African culture: that the dead ancestors, in a way, are not really dead, and that their exit from this world really provides them with the opportunity to look after the welfare of the living. In short, the dead constitute part of the universal cosmos.

Senghor similarly acknowledges the dead ancestors in 'Totem':

I must hide him in my innermost veins
The Ancestors whose stormy hide is shot
with lightning and thunder
My animal protector, I must hide him
That I may not break the barriers of scandal:
He is my faithful blood that demands fidelity
Protecting my naked pride against
Myself and the scorn of luckier races. (p. 50)

The phrase 'luckier races' alludes to the non-blacks, while the
word 'scorn' connotes the prejudice and derision in which the
coloured peoples are generally held in their encounter with them.
Senghor knows that the source of his power and safety derives
from the dead ancestors. But he is prudent, as custom demands,
to be covert about it. He must not disclose it. Such a disclosure,
he warns, borders on 'scandal'.

In 'Visit', Senghor salutes the memory of the dead ancestors
where through a dream he encounters certain departed souls: 'I
dream in the semi-darkness of an afternoon/I am visited by the
fatigues of the day/The deceased of the year ...' (p. 54); and in
'What Tempestuous Night' where he reminisces about some rituals
which are pertinent in mollifying the dead ancestors: 'And what
sacrifice will pacify the white masks of the goddess/Perhaps the
blood of chickens or goats, or the worthless blood of veins' (p. 55).

However, there are poems in which the celebrated dead are
not necessarily the benevolent parents, but those who, being
victims of disease, or war, or other human machinations, met their
untimely death. Senghor also praises their courage and heroism.
In 'The Dead', for instance, a piece apparently composed during
the aftermath of World War Two, Senghor opines that, although
the dead soldiers are victims of the evils of this world, they should
rest content that they have served humanity well. Besides, he
argues, they should feel satisfied that they died for the cause they
believed in:

They are lying out there beside the captured
roads, all along the roads of disaster
Elegant poplars, statues of sombre golds
draped in their long cloaks of gold

The great song of your blood will vanquish
machines and cannons

Your throbbing speech evasions and lies
No hate in your soul void of hatred, no
    cunning in your soul void of cunning
O Black Martyrs immortal race,
    let me speak words of pardon. (p. 53)

Senghor's second most important literary theme is the celebration of black beauty, which he articulates from several points
of view. Sometimes it involves his praise of African womanhood.
At other times it is one which acknowledges and celebrates the
beauty of the African continent in its interrelationships with
nature. And at still other times it is one which affords him the
opportunity to reminisce on Western civilisation *vis-à-vis* the indigenous culture, but leaving the reader to draw positive conclusions about his affinity for the latter.

The basis of Senghor's celebration of black beauty has a historical connection fuelled by the early Western misleading belief
that blackness is symptomatic of evil. Consequently, because
of this widespread belief, the black man was discriminated
against politically, socially and economically by other races who
associated blackness with ill-luck and negative human traits.
Colonialism and the slave trade, which exploited and dehuman-
ised the black man, only aggravated matters since he was not only
maltreated but conceived of as sub-human. It is partly to correct
this misleading impression of the black man, as well as restore his
own dignity, that Senghor in his poetry continually attributes
greatness and beauty to blackness.

In 'Night of Sine', Senghor praises the beauty of black womanhood. The African woman's 'hands' are 'gentler than fur', her
'breast glowing, like a Kuskus ball smoking out of the fire'. Her
sprightly gait and the dignity with which she carries herself are
suggested by the expression, 'The tall palmtrees swinging in the
nightwind/Hardly rustle' (p. 48). Perhaps no poem of Senghor's
better describes the physical attributes of the African woman,
and the poet's excitement about it, than 'I Will Pronounce Your
Name':

Naett, your name is mild like cinnamon, it is
    the fragrance in which the lemon grove sleeps,
Naett your name is the sugared clarity of
    blooming coffee trees

And it resembles the savannah, that blossoms forth
  under the masculine ardour of the midday sun.
Name of dew, fresher than the shadows
  of tamarind,
Fresher even than the short dusk, when the heat of
  the day is silenced.
Naett that is the dry tornado, the hard clap
  of lightning
Naett, coin of gold, shining coal,
  you my night, my sun! ... (p. 59)

But the African woman is more than just physically beautiful.
She is equally morally virtuous – faithful, devoted and loving. As
a manifestation of her love, she would, as in 'Be Not Amazed',
'weep in the twilight for the glowing voice that sang ... black
beauty' (p. 60). Senghor further highlights the African woman's
moral attributes in 'Night of Sine': she can 'light the lamp of clear
oil, and let the children/in bed talk about their ancestors, like their
parents' (p. 48). In short, the African woman is the embodiment
of hope, one upon whom the suffering youth can depend for
nourishment and growth.

In discussing the beauty of Africa, Senghor praises the excel-
lent qualities of its animate and inanimate objects, both living
and dead. In 'Night of Sine', for instance, the poet speaks of
'cradlesongs', the 'rhythmic silence' which 'rocks us'; he also talks
of the 'ancients of Elissa' and the 'shadowy visits of propitious
souls'. More than that, the scenery of the African landscape is
celestial:

This is the hour of the stars and of
  the night that dreams
And reclines on this hill of clouds, draped
  in her long gown of milk
The roofs of the houses gleam gently. What are
  they telling so confidently to the stars?
Inside the hearth is extinguished in the
  intimacy of bitter and sweet scents. (p. 48)

And where the poet contrasts the beauty of the indigenous culture
with the foreign landscape as in 'New York', the reader is left
in no doubt that the beauty of the former has a special place for
him:

New York! At first I was confused by your beauty,
    by those great golden long-legged girls
So shy at first before your blue metallic eyes,
    your frosted smile
So shy.

New York! I say to you: New York let
    black blood flow into your blood
That it may rub the rust from your steel
    joints, like an oil of life,
That it may give to your bridges the bend
    of buttocks and the suppleness of creepers. (pp. 56, 58)

In the poems in which he treats the theme of Western exploitation of Africa, without attacking the Western ways, he docu-
ments his aversion to the ravages of colonialism, the slave trade,
and neo-colonialism in their various ramifications. The basis of
Senghor's abhorrence of colonial exploitation can be found in his
wide educational background and his sense of justice. As Abiola
Irele observes, 'Senghor rejects the idea that the black man is
inferior in his human quality to the white man.'[6]

True, Senghor believes in a just society, a society in which
everyone can develop his potentialities to the fullest. But he knows
that the black man has not been able to do this because of the
coloniser's conquest of his innate will through technology. In 'New
York' Senghor remonstrates: 'Listen New York! Oh listen to your
male voice of brass/vibrating with oboes, the anguish choked with
tears/falling in great clots of blood' (p. 57). In 'Luxembourgh 1939',
he laments: 'Europe is burying the yeast of nations and the hope
of/newer races' (p. 50).

In 'Paris in the Snow', Senghor highlights the devastating
effects of colonialism. He recalls:

The white hands that loaded the guns that
    destroyed the kingdoms,
The hands that whipped the slaves and
    that whipped you
The dusty hands that slapped you, the
    white powdered hands that slapped me
The sure hands that pushed me into
    solitude and hatred
The white hands that felled the high forest
    that dominated Africa,

That felled the Saras, erect and firm
  in the heart of Africa, beautiful like
  the first men that were
  created by your brown hands.
They felled the virgin forest to turn
  into railway sleepers.
They felled Africa's forest in order
  to save civilization that was lacking in men.
Lord, I can still not abandon this last hate,
I know it, the hatred of diplomats
  who show their long teeth
And who will barter with black flesh tomorrow. (p. 51)

The above lines are crucial in appreciating the black man's past
and present. They also underscore the colonialist's operative
mechanism. For example, while the past for the black man is
symbolised by 'Kingdoms' and 'virgin forest', the present is suggested by 'slavery', 'solitude and hatred'. 'Guns' symbolises the
colonialist's instrument of dehumanisation suggested by the verbs
'destroyed', 'whipped', 'slapped', 'pushed', and 'fell'. Interestingly
Senghor does not employ invective in dealing with the theme of
colonialism; rather he is content to be ironical in documenting
grave human situations. Thus, events, when viewed carefully and
closely, suggest a negative sequence of Western colonialism:
exploitation, hypocrisy, stasis.

Coming now to Senghor's final theme, which centres on the
spirit of reconciliation, it is important to say that two possible
reasons can be adduced for the presence of this theme in
Senghor's verse. First, as the foremost African writer who has
suffered most severely from the evil effects of colonialism and
from World War Two – he was held captive by the German forces
between 1940 and 1943 – he is in a better position to appreciate
the adage which says that two wrongs cannot make a right by
practising revenge. Second, having risen to the presidency of his
country he not only had the unique opportunity to practise the
ideals of statesmanship, which include tolerance and forebear-
ance, but was better exposed to the problems posed by diverse
elements from diverse cultural backgrounds and thus would
rather encourage the spirit of cooperation and unity among them
for the ultimate good of mankind.

Among Senghor's poems which focus on the theme of reconciliation are 'In Memoriam', 'Paris in the Snow' and 'Prayer to Masks'. In 'Paris in the Snow', Senghor draws the reader's attention to the national motto displayed in the capital city and captioned, 'Peace to all men of goodwill', apparently to underscore the hypocrisy of such public displays but more importantly to suggest his own personal belief in such an ideal. At the end of the poem he adds that his life's principle is anchored on being 'kind to my enemies, my brothers with the snowless/white hands' (p. 51). The interesting thing here is the corresponding equation of 'enemies' with 'brothers'. By implication the colonialists are not to be seen simply as 'enemies', but 'brothers' as well, who deserve kind consideration and forgiveness.

'In Memoriam' also speaks of 'my brothers with stony faces' and of the persona's eagerness 'To join my brothers with blue eyes/With hard hands'. The irony here is predicated on the fact that one would have thought that the poet would be scared by those who misuse others through their own cruelty. On the contrary he prays to understand them as a phenomenon and, apparently, to appreciate their universe. As a poetic metaphor for reconciliation, 'join' indicates the degree to which the poet is ready to spread the gospel of reconciliation and brotherly love among people.

'Prayer to Masks' is a projection of the diverse racial groups which, due to certain ineluctable forces, converge in France: 'Black mask, red mask, you black and white masks,/ Rectangular masks through whom the spirit breathes' (p. 53). The poem's symbolism is clear enough: all human beings come from the same source and will ultimately retire to the grave. Paris is here only the melting pot. The allusion recalls Donne's epithet of 'Nature's Nest of Boxes'.

Appropriately the employment of the plural form 'Masks' vis-à-vis 'Prayer' in the poem's title, suggests the poet's reverence for the past sages of all nationalities who have traversed this earth. Senghor emphasises his belief in the brotherhood of all races: 'Europe' and 'Africa' are 'connected through the navel'. These two continents symbolise the world's diverse racial elements, while 'navel' suggests the link between the complex of life and death through which all human beings must pass. Thus there is the need, the poet seems to say, for all men to be united, to be reconciled to one another even in the face of discord and hate.

What can we now conclude about Senghor's contribution to Negritude and to African poetry in general? Firstly, he pioneered the founding of a socio-cultural and literary movement which championed the promotion of Africa's cultural values. Secondly he was, through his writing and inspiration, a fighter for black rights and human freedom and dignity. And finally, Senghor's poems and the themes they articulate – the dead ancestors, black beauty and African womanhood, colonialism, and of course reconciliation – are not only basic topics of interest in African poetics, but also they offer the reader an opportunity to visualise how Senghor's practical humanity as poet corresponds with his practical humanity as philosopher-statesman.

While Senghor can be described as a literary liberal in terms of his philosophy of life and his aesthetic credo, David Diop's work epitomises agitation and radicalism in its entirety. David Diop's only volume of poetry, *Coups de pilon*, published during his lifetime, voices cynicism and bitterness against an age threatened by racism, colonialism, exploitation and war.

Born in Bordeaux, France, in 1927 to a Senegalese father and a Cameroonian mother, David Diop spent most of his life in France but because he was often ill, he visited Africa frequently in order to improve his failing health. Unfortunately he died in 1960 in an air crash off Dakar at the age of 33.

During his lifetime, David Diop recorded bitter memories connected with racism and the Second World War. He was also nostalgic about Africa which features prominently in his poetry. Whereas one finds in Senghor an abiding faith in the positive values of both European and African cultures, David Diop's work demonstrates outright and total denunciation and rejection of colonialism and Western civilisation. O. R. Dathorne explains why his poetic ethos contrasts sharply with that of his Negritude contemporaries:

> David Diop lived during the time when negritude was in its infancy and he died at an early age. His *Coup de pilon* (1956) expresses the anger of Césaire, for he was born in France and only visited Africa. He therefore has more in common with the West Indians and less in common with Senghor and Birago Diop.[7]

Three major Negritude themes recur in David Diop's poetry: criticism of Western civilisation and its attendant colonialism;

nostalgia for and glorification of Africa; and firm belief in a future Africa which is prosperous, united and strong.

The most dominant of these themes in David Diop's verse is his attack on Western civilisation. In his treatment of this theme, his attitude recalls on the one hand that of McKay's – assertive, militant and defiant; on the other hand that of Kofi Awoonor's – bitter, mocking and sarcastic.

His uncompromising indictment of Western civilisation arises from the fact that it is the source of many human woes: slavery, alienation and exploitation. Through Western civilisation the African was conquered in body and spirit by the colonialist who misused his talents in the mines and plantations; in the Western world the enslaved African or Negro was alienated both from his fatherland and from the mainstream of other races with whom he interacted; the conquered African was exploited not only in the West but also in his fatherland where his cash crops, minerals, and other natural resources were siphoned away into foreign lands. In short, the lot of the African in his relationships with his conqueror was no better than what Richard Wright describes as 'race hate, rejection, ignorance . . . murder, fiery crosses and fear'.[8] All these constitute much of the bitterness in David Diop's work.

In 'Africa' the poet notes that during its pristine days Africa was renowned for its brave and heroic leaders, its fertile lands, and for its great agricultural potentials. With the onset of Western colonialism, however, the continent was not only looted, its citizens were brutalised and subjugated beyond recognition. He laments:

Africa tell me Africa
Is this you this back that is bent
This back that breaks under the
     weight of humiliation
This back trembling with red scars? (p. 63)

In 'Listen Comrades', the poet, with restrained emotion, discusses how death dogged the path of the indigenous population during the era of the slave trade. In their mad rush to exploit the African continent and enslave its people, the colonial powers killed the local citizenry in great numbers. Not even the aged ones were spared. 'Mamba with his white hairs' was also killed; for the poet, he symbolises all those who suffered death and persecution in the hands of the colonialists. But rather than give in to despair and cynicism, the poet stoically exhorts the local people to look forward to a future filled with hope and freedom attainable through their own spirited struggle.

Of all David Diop's poems, 'The Vultures' represents his most sarcastic and satirical work in terms of delineating the evil and ugliness of Western colonialism. It is also probably his most famous single poem. The poem is significant in the sense that it is one of the few African lyrics in which animal or bird imagery is employed to dramatise human behaviour.

In this piece the poet draws a character sketch of the colonialist symbolised as the vulture, a predatory, sinister bird. Unlike Kofi Awoonor's 'The Weaverbird' where the poem continually draws the reader's attention to the character of the weaverbird in its ingratitude, here in 'The Vultures' the poet does not allude to the bird in the body of the poem but leaves the reader to draw his own conclusions by comparing the poem's title with what is discussed in the entire piece. The interesting thing here is that Diop allows the narrative to develop unobtrusively while relying on the imaginative ability of the reader to appreciate the poem's moral import.

The poem is couched in irony: the colonialist is the architect of Christianity, yet he 'did not know love'. He preaches civilisation, yet he breaks all moral codes through 'exhorted kisses/Of promises broken at the point of a gun'. In this poem, colonialism is vigorously assailed because it is the embodiment of human oppression, religious hypocrisy, and economic domination.

As a satiric allegory the piece dramatises the negative aspect of human nature. The vulture, for example, surreptitiously preys on its victims on whose carcasses it feeds. By implication the colonialist comes to Africa, not as a friend, but as an enemy. The employment of the images 'kicked', 'slapped', and 'bloodstained monument of tutelage', help to underscore the wickedness and brutality of the colonialist in his worst elements.

The poet's sense of nostalgia, his second theme, arises from his often long absence from the African continent. Also fuelling this theme was his proneness to illness, which inspired his yearning to return home in order to improve his health, or more realistically, to reflect on those times when he lived and enjoyed the comfort and beauty of his boyhood days in Africa. In 'Africa' he laments:

Africa my Africa
Africa of proud warriors in
    ancestral savannahs
Africa of whom my grandmother sings
I have never known you
But your blood flows in my veins. (p. 63)

Yet in 'Your Presence' he writes with exultation:

In your presence I rediscovered my name
My name that was hidden under the
    pain of separation
I rediscovered the eyes no longer
    veiled with fever
And your laughter like a flame
    piercing the shadows
Has revealed Africa to me beyond
    the snows of yesterday. (p. 62)

Nothing better dramatises the poet's affinity and love for Africa than the above two passages. In the first passage, the repetitive employment of the epithet 'Africa' not only demonstrates his love of it, but suggests the poet's desire to be part and parcel of the African world-view. Also contributing to the poem's effectiveness is the imagery, 'your blood flows in my veins', which shows how, committed in body and spirit, an intense emotional feeling wells up in the poet the moment he recognises he is re-united with his people. As it were, the agonising 'fever' and 'separation', which apparently affect his psyche, are submerged by the sense of 'laughter' and joy which Africa means to him.

He also captures the mood of the Negress and Negro who, like him, are exiled in foreign lands. This is especially demonstrated in the poems 'To A Black Dancer' and 'Nigger Tramp', pieces which depict the pitiful condition of these exiles and of their hopeful wish to return to their fatherland.

In 'To A Black Dancer' the poet extols the beauty of the Negress and the wonderful effect this beauty has on him: Her 'breasts and sacred powers', her 'naked . . . smile', her 'magic . . . loins', her 'myths' – all 'burn around me' (p. 65). The beauty and grace of the

Negress remind him of Africa of old against a background of the new:

> You are the idea of All and the
>   voice of the Ancient
> Gravely rocketed against our fears
> You are the Word which explodes
> In showers of light upon the
>   shores of oblivion. (p. 65)

In 'Nigger Tramp' the poet catalogues the misery and woes of the Negro, whose ordeals recall the 'bitter ways' of the slaves in the 'mines' and 'cornfields'. Not even the descendants of the slaves are given their due respect for 'They called you Half-White' (p. 66). While narrating the miserable life of the Negro, the poem draws our attention to the peace and warmth of Africa.

When we come to his final theme – that is, his belief in a future Africa that is united, progressive, and strong – it is important to emphasise the fact that virtually all of his poems end on an optimistic note couched in a simple resolution, as in 'Africa':

> In spendid loneliness amidst white
>   and faded flowers
> That is Africa your Africa
> That grows again patiently obstinately
> And its fruit gradually acquire
> The bitter taste of liberty. (p. 64)

'Listen Comrades':

> It is the sign of the dawn
> The sign of brotherhood which comes
>   to nourish the dreams of men. (p. 62)

and 'The Vultures':

> In spite of the desolate villages
>   of torn Africa
> Hope was preserved in us as in
>   a fortress
> And from the mines of Swaziland to
>   the factories of Europe
> Spring will be reborn under our bright steps. (p. 64)

Two interesting things stand out strongly from the above passages. Firstly, is his strong awareness of the ephemeral nature of Western colonialism which strengthens his resolve and hope for the future. Secondly, by projecting a note of optimism against a general background of injustice, the poet portrays himself as a far more sensitive and mature individual than the colonialists.

On a more general note it can be said that the success of his work is due not only to the fact that it symbolises, as Roscoe says, 'the extremist voice of negritude',[9] but perhaps more importantly the fact that in treating his themes, he continually attaches enormous significance to the future state of an oppressed people and their prospects for survival against inimical odds.

Of the Negritude poets under study in this article, Birago Diop is the most consistently devoted to the theme of African culture and tradition. It is this singular theme, perhaps more than anything else, that distinguishes his verse. Although he inveighs against those who foolishly copy Western civilisation, and although he repudiates European colonialism, these themes are greatly subterranean to his celebration of the indigenous culture.

Born in Dakar in 1906, he was a veterinary surgeon by profession. Birago Diop was brought up by educated parents who early in life inspired his interest in African mythology and folklore, a fact which apparently accounts for the predominance of African lore in his work. A highly talented man, his poetic output is not prodigious but skilled. He was a widely travelled man, having spent much of his life in what was then Upper Volta, where he worked in the government civil service. He also travelled in France where, apart from receiving his higher education, he came to be closely associated with Damas and Senghor with whom he founded the Negritude literary movement.

Of Birago Diop's three themes – that is, his treatment of Western colonialism in Africa, his criticism of those who foolishly imitate the Western lifestyle, and his celebration of the indigenous culture, the first stands out. The poet treats the theme of Western colonialism in 'Omen' and 'Ball'.

The poem 'Omen', which critics have generally ignored, describes the state of Africa through its respective stanzas at three stages – pre-colonialism, colonialism, colonialism and after – employing, at every stage, diverse images and symbols to develop its thesis:

A naked sun – a yellow sun
A sun all naked at early dawn
Pours waves of gold over the bank
Of the river of yellow.

A naked sun – a white sun
A sun all naked and white
Pours waves of silver
Over the river of white

A naked sun – a red sun
A sun all naked and red
Pours waves of red blood
Over the river of red. (p. 69)

The first stanza, which describes the period before the coming of the colonialists, sees Africa in its prosperous state waxing strong in 'gold'. The second stanza sees it degenerate into 'silver', apparently due to the coloniser's excessive exploitation of the continent. The third stanza perceives the entire dislocation of the continent, culminating in the clamour for independence and the subsequent wave of fighting and bloodshed arising from the attempt to wrest freedom from the coloniser.

Apart from the images suggested through the epithets 'gold', 'silver', and 'red blood', the poem employs colours as symbols to enunciate a fundamental moral. Thus the 'yellow sun' shines on the 'river of yellow', the 'white sun' on the 'river of white', while the 'red sun' reflects on the 'river of red'. By implication the poem articulates the universal philosophical belief that good begets good, while evil results in disaster.

Traditionally the colours have had different connotations and meanings depending on the occasion and the circumstance. For example, yellow is alluring, but sometimes suggests a decline and here in the arrival of the colonialists is heavy with foreboding.

White suggests attractiveness and purity, as well as death. Thus the arrival of the colonialist, although initially promising, signifies impending doom. The irony here is that the attractiveness and apparent innocence of this colour can deceive its victim into making costly mistakes. The African was misled into believing in the good intention of the colonialists but ultimately paid dearly for it.

Red conjures up evil or danger; conjoined with 'blood' it depicts the last phase of European colonialism characterised by destruction and death.

In the refrain 'A sun all naked', 'sun' is a metaphor for Africa while the epithet 'naked' suggests the innocence and purity of the continent. Africa's open nakedness is the cause of both its attractiveness to, and its violation by the coloniser.

On the surface the title of the poem 'Ball' connotes the soccer ball; but on a deeper, reflective level, it symbolises the trickery and hypocrisy which are part and parcel of Western colonialism whose attendant evils are further signalled in 'secret accord', 'vague promises', all culminating in 'sobs and tears', and 'a heavy regret'.

According to the poet, the colonisers infiltrated themselves into Africa, some as Christians, others signing pacts with the local leaders or flattering them with gifts such as 'perfumes' or gunpowder. Ultimately, the gullible African loses. In a harsh, austere tone, Diop orders the coloniser to desist from his atrocities:

Stop jazz, you scan the sobs and tears
That jealous hearts keep only to themselves,
Stop your scrap-iron din. Your uproar
Seems like a huge complaint where
consent is born. (p. 70)

His second theme, the criticism of Africans who 'copy' Western civilisation, appears in 'Vanity'. Whether it is the modern-day worship of materialism, or the practice of celebrating the Western lifestyle which some African's regard as 'sophistication', Birago sees these as vanity.

In a veiled and implicit mood, rather mock-heroic, the poet alludes to those who deviate from society's cherished norms as 'beggars' with 'large mouths' and 'pitiful anger/which grows ... like a tumour'. Nothing better dramatises the poet's contempt for this category of people than the phrase 'blind deaf and unworthy sons' (p. 70).

All through the poem (including its title which is apparently taken from the Book of Ecclesiastes 1: 2), he exposes the negative aspect of those who see nothing good in their own traditional background: they would end up, he says, with fruitless 'cries', 'wild appeals', 'clamourings' and 'sobbing hearts' (p. 70).

Birago Diop's most dominant theme, the celebration of the indigenous culture, apart from emphasising the place of ritual sacrifice in traditional African culture, underscores the belief among the local citizenry that without the support and active cooperation of the dead ancestors, the living cannot achieve success. In 'Viaticum' he effectively chronicles the ritual sacrifice which the initiate has to make in his community if he is to overcome the trials and tribulations of this world.

The word 'viaticum' is employed apparently as a parody of the Catholic Christian mode of preparing the dying for his last journey on earth. The poem is divided into three stanzas. The first stanza introduces us to the significance of the dead ancestors in human affairs and proceeds to give an account of the symbolic role of the word 'three' in traditional ritual setting (e.g., 'three pots', 'three fingers').

Stanza two, apart from highlighting the role played by one's mother, describes the specific objects used in performing the ritual ceremony – 'dog's blood', 'bull's blood', and 'goat's blood'. It also emphasises certain important aspects of the ritual sacrifice: e.g., the fact that 'Mother' has to annoint the initiate's body, particularly the 'forehead', the 'breast', and the 'navel'; the fact that the sacrifice is performed during the period of the 'full Moon'; and the fact that three fingers of the initiate's right hand – the thumb, the index and the next – are to be held up in the direction of the North, East, South, and West during the sacrifice. It is in this stanza too that the 'Mother' gives her full blessing to the initiate, assuring him of the full protection of the dead ancestors.

Stanza three, the concluding stanza, is the initiate's personal soliloquy; he announces to the audience that, with the sacrifice performed, he is insured against the hazards of this world:

Since then I go
I follow the pathways
the pathways and roads
beyond the sea and even farther,
beyond the sea and beyond the beyond;
And whenever I approach the wicked,
the Men with black hearts,
whenever I approach the envious,
the Men with black hearts
before me moves the Breath of the Ancestors. (p. 72)

Besides the naming of specific objects to underscore their significance, he employs repetition in the poem for rhythmic effect and for emphasis:

I too held my fingers red with blood,
with dog's blood,
with bull's blood,
with goat's blood. (p. 71)

These lines evoke both active and passive responses to intensify meaning. And in order to communicate his message effectively, he uses simple and lucid diction. Finally the poem is emotive, for apart from employing such metaphors as 'blood', 'breast', 'navel', and 'forehead' – metaphors that touch on the very foundations of our existence – the entire piece highlights the depth of feeling, courage and expiation which characterise African ritual ceremonies.

In the poem 'Vanity', although the poet inveighs against all those who imitate the Western lifestyle, the poem essentially directs our attention to the need to celebrate traditional cultural values, particularly the dead ancestors. The consequences for failing to do this, the poet laments, would be unfortunate:

When our Dead come with their Dead
When they have spoken to us with
their clumsy voices;
Just as our ears were deaf
To their cries, to their wide appeals

Just as our ears were deaf
They have left on the earth their cries,
In the air, on the water, where they
have traced their signs
For us, blind deaf and unworthy Sons
Who see nothing of what they have made
In the air, on the water, where they have
traced their signs

And since we did not understand our Dead
Since we have never listened to their cries
If we weep, gently, gently
If we cry roughly of our torments
What heart will listen to our clamourings
What ear to our sobbing hearts? (p. 70)

Two questions arise the first is, what unique contributions distinguish these poets as Negritudists? The second is, what impact has Negritude, as a literary movement, had on African literature, particularly poetry?

My answer to the first question is: Whereas Senghor believes strongly in the spirit of reconciliation and the celebration of the dead ancestors, and while David Diop acidly attacks European colonialism for exploiting Africa, Birago Diop can be said to be a *via media* between these extreme positions of his contemporaries, in that while not preaching reconciliation nor openly condemning Western civilisation, at the same time he demonstrates his sensitivity to the evils of European colonialism while glorifying African cultural values.

My response to the second question is: Negritude is important in African aesthetics, for, apart from adding to the African literary vocabulary, it is one of the very few formalised literary movements in African literature. Finally, Negritude has provided Senghor, David Diop, and Birago Diop - the three greatest African Negritude poets - with the literary resource or tool with which to fashion their poetry, and has fostered a healthy critical debate among critics of African literature.

NOTES

1. As cited by Taban lo Liyong in *The Last Word* (Nairobi: East African Publishing House, 1969) 24.
2. Aimé Césaire, in *Return to my Native Land* (London: Penguin, 1969) 2.
3. Eldred D. Jones, 'The Essential Soyinka', in *Introduction to Nigerian Literature*, ed. Bruce King (London: University of Lagos and Evans Brothers Ltd, 1971) 113.
4. Gerald Moore and Ulli Beier, *Modern Poetry from Africa* (Harmondsworth: Penguin Books Ltd, 1978) 17. All poem citations from the poetry of Léopold Sédar Senghor, David Diop and Birago Diop are from this edition and are incorporated in the text, followed by the page number(s).
5. See Senghor, 'The Struggle for Negritude', in *Senghor: Prose and Poetry*, ed. J. Reed and C. Wake (London: Oxford University Press, 1965) 97. For detailed studies on the origin and background of Negritude, see: Abiola Irele, *The African Experience in Literature and Ideology* (London and Ibadan: Heinemann, 1981) 67-116; Oladele Taiwo, *An Introduction to West African Literature* (London: Thomas Nelson and Sons Ltd, 1967) 43-53; O. R. Dathorne,

African Literature in the Twentieth Century (London: Heinemann, 1979) 217-48.

6. Abiola Irele, *The African Experience in Literature and Ideology* (London: Heinemann Educational Books, 1981) 71.

7. O. R. Dathorne, *African Literature in the Twentieth Century* (London and Ibadan: Heinemann, 1979) 235.

8. Richard Wright, *White Man, Listen* (New York: Doubleday, 1957) 76.

9. Adrian Roscoe, *Mother is Gold: A Study in West African Literature* (London and New York: Cambridge University Press, 1977) 3.

Pidgin Literature, Criticism & Communication

Ezenwa-Ohaeto

Communication is at the core of literature and pidgin literature demonstrates the essence of this communication through the utilisation of relevant literary devices. However, in order to assimilate and disseminate ideas it is necessary for each literature to generate its own critical theory, produce enough works to justify it or succumb to the threat of extinction. This task was accomplished by African literature in the sixties as more works written by Africans became widely accepted. It is no longer fashionable to ask even in Europe: 'What is African Literature?' Feminist criticism is gradually accomplishing this task despite the plurality of the critical works produced and their, sometimes, contradictory postulations.

The statement made by Chinua Achebe while the controversy surrounding African literature was raging is worth recollecting:

> The European critic of African literature must cultivate the habit of humility appropriate to his limited experience of the *African* world and purged of the superiority and arrogance which history so insidiously makes him heir to. (Achebe: 6)

That statement was restructured by Mineke Schipper in order to reflect the necessity for reassessing women and literature in Africa and she quotes it thus:

> The *male* critic of African literature must cultivate the habit of humility appropriate to his limited experience of the *female* world and purged of the superiority and arrogance which history so insidiously makes him heir to. (Schipper: 55)

It is pertinent to rephrase that same quotation in order to illustrate the need for the generation of an appropriate critical theory for pidgin literature. A restructuring of the comment would read thus:

> The *elitist* critic of African literature must cultivate the habit of humility appropriate to his limited experience of the *pidgin* world and purged of the superiority and arrogance which history so insidiously makes him heir to.

The point highlighted in this quotation clearly situates the issue which this essay seeks to discuss. It is the need for a cultivation of appropriate theoretical approaches to the analysis of pidgin literature which makes communication its primary role. The essay thus seeks to establish that the paucity of critical commentaries and also the problem of misinterpretation of pidgin literature are the consequences of limited critical experience and the inordinate desire to impose the critic's limitations on a work of literature. This essay does not seek to dictate the only routes through which pidgin literature could be discussed but to generate ideas that could be utilised in the formulation of critical theories.

The variety inherent in the literature in English constantly produced in many parts of the world requires a variety of critical approaches. This is why one critic has postulated that 'the challenge the post-colonial literatures pose is that of re-thinking the organisation and function of knowledge' (Brydon: 93). The re-thinking involved in the critical analysis of pidgin literature requires a fair knowledge of the world-view expressed in it. This world-view may appear similar to that of the writer using standard English but it is well known that there are certain phrases in pidgin that embody a concept different from even the word which originated it. This injunction is necessary for quite often many critics regard pidgin expressions as either a nuisance in a work of formal English literature or an exotic literary item.

This idea needs to be explained. A consideration of Saro-Wiwa's *Sozaboy* which is a potpourri of pidgin, broken English and occasional flashes of good, even idiomatic English, indicates several words that embody a philosophy of life unavailable to the mainstream critic of African literature (Saro-Wiwa: 82–166). The expressions: 'knacktory' (gossip or tell stories); 'making yanga' (being unduly proud); 'palaver' (trouble); 'wuruwuru' (chicanery or cheating); 'ashewo' (prostitute); 'drink don begin turn-turn for my eye' (getting tipsy); 'helele' (throughly or properly); 'ye-ye man' (ne'er do well); 'take make small cooleh' (enjoy oneself with); 'woman rapa' (womaniser); 'make gra-gra' (be unduly quarrelsome); 'water don pass garri' (matters have come to a crisis); 'whackies' (food); 'tory don worwor' (the worst has happened) all possess significations that may not be effectively discussed unless the critic has access to the philosophy that originated those expressions. Thus it is essential for the critic of pidgin literature to modify the terms of reference through which African literature has traditionally been discussed.

It is necessary to add that one is not making this analysis merely out of the desire to prevent an invasion of one's turf but one is writing with the insight generated by the experience of being a practitioner – a creative writer and a critic. One cannot object to the attempts to incorporate a critical discussion of pidgin literature into the realm of formal African literature but one is bothered by an uncritical assumption that since pidgin literature arouses humour, it then becomes its *only* enduring quality. A notable African critic warns against this tendency in the seventies when he concludes that 'the functions of criticism to literature, audience and society are legion. In all cases some consideration for the text is essential; but no single critical orientation can be adequate. The best we can do is to discourage the complacency of simple attitudes and the tyranny of uniformity' (Izevbaye: 17). It is this tyranny of uniformity and simplistic approach to pidgin literature which one seeks to discourage.

Among the objectives of the critic of pidgin literature is the desire to utilise experience in order to understand the philosophical, technical and cultural underpinnings of pidgin literature. The impulse to utilise an all-embracing theory which never took pidgin literature into consideration in its formulation is flawed by the misleading emphasis that it must possess a similarity to the patterns already in existence. The critical view must be able to accommodate the possibility of originality in differences from established patterns. But it is known that this method may not be isolated for there is that critical zone where all theories inevitably converge in African literature and it is the zone of relevance because African literature has not imbibed the excesses of art for art's sake, since the peculiarity of the conflicts and tension in its developing countries that inform some of those exciting literatures in existence, may be similar. The argument is not that language has made a difference in experience but that language makes a difference in the concept of experience.

There is the need to look closely at pidgin texts responding to what the writer has set down rather than scanning the work and making general commentaries that often originate from the critics distorted views. This close reading of pidgin literature agrees with the demands of practical criticism because 'the words on the page function not in isolation but in relation to one another and even the most spontaneous and unconscious of artist structures his or her work to produce a total effect. The words on the page are generally intended to convey meaning through form; the exercise of practical criticism seeks to identify not only the writer's meaning but also the often largely hidden structure that is ultimately what gives the text its impact on the reader' (Wake: 6). The product of detailed analysis which this exercise generates means that pidgin literature would yield its juices to the benefit of the critic, reader and literature.

Practical criticism does not function in isolation and it is not bereft of theories but the essential aspect is that it should be rooted in the literary work and that its critical derivations must be justified by textual content. The foisting of a particular literary theory introduces conflicts and those conflicts may represent amplifications of positions that have been long established. Perhaps this is why it has been argued that 'the significant division in African literary theory is not that between various 'schools' or techniques in the so-called 'marketplace' of divergent methodologies – between, for example, 'historical' and 'textualist' strategies. On the contrary, it is to be found in what I shall call the Fanonist 'threshold' that divides 'accommodation' with existing Western textual strategies and rejection of Eurocentric methodologies in the search for an Afrocentric means of reading and understanding texts' (Berger: 142). The critical discussion of the poems, plays and prose works in pidgin thus requires a further immersion in an Afrocentric concept which takes into consideration all of its dimensions.

The arguments that raged in the early stages of African literature, which are now raging in the discussions concerning feminism in literature are bound to be re-stated if pidgin literature is to be appreciated. The debate is no longer a question of its acceptability but the inculcation of a correct critical attitude. An examination of the characteristics of pidgin especially its humour and wit emphasises the need for the adoption of relevant critical attitudes. In a review of my collection of poems in both formal English and pidgin, a reviewer states that 'while the poems written in formal English belong to the best traditions of good poetry by virtue of superior emotionality of subject matter, lucid language and moderate tone, those written in pidgin English appear unwieldingly wobbly and are saved only by the light-heartedness bestowed by the lingual medium' (Shaka: 37). The connotation which this comment implies is that the 'light-heartedness' or the humour is an end in itself rather than a means to an end. This critical attitude does not take into consideration the fact that humour could be fashioned to be ironic, meta-phorically symbolic or simply a means to enhance the creative focus of the work. In pidgin literature, however, the use of humour is intrinsic but it differs according to the purpose of the writer. The humour in Frank Aig-Imoukhuede's *Pidgin Stew and Suffer-head* differs from the humour in Mamman Vatsa's *Tori for Geti Bowleg* and both differ from the humour in Segun Oyekunle's *Katakata for Sufferhead* and Tunde Fatunde's *Oga Na Tief-Man, Water No Get Enemy, No Food No Country* and *Blood and Sweat*.

However, the critical view where the humour is seen only as a veneer could be misleading in most instances. In addition, the fact that pidgin literature makes use of abundant humour also creates the impression that it is not serious. This attitude is also reflected in works in formal English where humourous and entertaining writers are not accorded critical respect because it is believed that accessibility in communication is related to inferior crafts-manship. A well known European writer who observed this atti-tude comments that 'if a book is hard going, it ought to be good. If it posits a complex moral situation it ought to be even better. If it has a multitude of *sous-textes* and a battery of symbols it is supreme fodder for doctoral theses and the stuff of tenure. To be a mere entertainer is not enough. And yet to entertain is far more difficult than to enlighten' (Burgess: 16). The idea is that entertain-ment or the arousal of humour is not easy to accomplish which means that there are certain deliberate creative efforts made to arouse that effect.

Humour enables the writer in pidgin to explore social reality insightfully and interestingly, because it is achieved through the use of hilarious allusions, ironic perceptions, succinct imagery and the tabulations of incongruities in human behaviour. These comic structures vary according to the creative powers of each writer but they must not be perceived as an end in themselves despite the fascinating mode of the presentations. Humour should be seen as part of the creative quality that has heightened the communicatory aspects of pidgin literature. Thus a critical theory adopted by a critic of pidgin literature should take it into consideration.

Another critic insists that 'an apparent danger in pidgin poetry is to slide into the world-view of the man in the street or the girl next door' (Omoifo: 79). This observation does not seem clear because the man in the street or the girl next door could be highly articulate and responsive to the events in the world. Actually what that critic is implying is that the world-view of the man in the street or the girl next door is banal and pedestrian. However, the fact that the writers in pidgin are not operating under academic constraints but out of choice, means that the use of pidgin will always be channelled through the forge of the writer's personal experience, awareness of literary devices and individual imaginative powers. These writers are also aware of what the poet Tanure Ojaide means when he argues that 'languages get old and worn-out as human beings and other things, and consequently they lose their colour and vigour. Non-native English as in Nigeria is still fresh, exciting and vigorous. It has no inhibitions. It accommodates syntactical and other grammatical distortions'. The writer in pidgin could create some of these grammatical and syntactical distortions deliberately in order to respond artistically to an experience. In effect the awareness or even the use of the world-view of the man in the street or the girl next door need not be a disadvantage and it could be used to enhance the creative focus of the work of literature in pidgin through the adoption of an ironic perception of reality.

All the same, an aspect of literature in pidgin which has generated much discussion is the view that in terms of communication it is overtly accessible. In a comment in a national daily, one of its arts writers feels that:

Where pidgin comes in we can think both in purely aesthetic and utilitarian terms. One would conjecture that while one of our pioneer poets, Frank Aig-Imoukhuede explores the language for its near natural appeal and perhaps because if effectively contrived it will stimulate some nuances of the indigenous language, the new dimension waxes towards the use-value of poetry so expressed in pidgin. So much of poetry in pidgin now tends to defuse the ossified thoughts embedded in poetry in Queen's English. The poetic licence is applied, knocking down the barriers of diction to attend to immediate social questions. There is an urge to be practically involved in a populist dialogue for socio-political resolutions. There is a wish to put linguistic alienation behind. There is the need to create a new bard shorn of academic pretences [relied] upon by the curious masses for a few explanations to their existence. All these speak for the use-value to which, one believes, critics will soon attend. (Tomoloju: 11)

The needs that were pointed out in the above quotation are real. But the insistence of Ben Tomoloju that the use-value (the utilitarian aspect) is what is emphasised by pidgin poetry (or pidgin literature) is not correct. The varied degrees to which the writers emphasise the content of their works and the variation in their choices of devices imply that the aesthetic aspects cannot be ignored. It should be reiterated that content without form is unsatisfactory while form without content makes a work irrelevant. The critical theory which can adequately serve the requirements of pidgin literature must emphasise both form and content. It should also start with a careful examination of individual works as a notable critic in an interview with Kalu Ogbaa reminds us when he asserts that 'we need a lot of scholarship to begin with. Each novel, poem or play needs to be patiently described with regard to its rhetoric, its verbal texture, its form, its background, its significance' (Ogbaa: 103).

There is the need for this patient description, assessment and analysis of pidgin literature so that its ability to communicate is not seen from the wrong perspective. It is clear that some of the issues predominant in pidgin literature now would diminish with time as Abiola Irele observed in the early days of African literature: 'the social factor was important only because the literature itself was largely sociological. As the literature becomes less preoccupied with social or national problems and more concerned with the problems of men as individuals in an African society, the critical reference will be human beings rather than society, and the consideration which influences critical judgement will be human and literary rather than social ones', (Irele: 30). All the same, the current trends in pidgin literature can only be assessed if the critic is aware of the extent of productivity and if he is also aware of Ernest Emenyonu's injunction that a critic has 'an obligation to his society – he is a kind of guide and teacher to them but it becomes somewhat of an irony when he proves the judge of what more intelligent and sensitive people are reading' (Emenyonu: 29). Although our argument stresses the need for a proper attitude of respect to the creative work in pidgin, we accept the critical attitude that 'any literature needs all the criticism it can get. Only by glimpsing truth from a variety of perspectives are we able to comprehend its complexities and ambiguities. Only by comparing different views of the same subject can we arrive at a valid conception of what it really looks like. If we choose to stand still and see everything through rose-coloured spectacles, we will have a narrow, tainted vision of reality' (Lindfors: 54).

The conclusion is that in as much as a myopic critical view is discouraged the critic must not pronounce conclusions that are not justified. Literature can only be adequately and relevantly developed if the critics are aware of its intrinsic qualities and if they are not misled by its ability to communicate easily. When proper critical attitudes are adopted it will become obvious that pidgin literature is a literature of communication which incorporates utilitarian and aesthetic qualities that could enable it to entertain, educate, intellectualise, moralise and acculturate.

WORKS CITED

Achebe Chinua. *Morning Yet on Creation Day*, (London: Heinemann, 1975).

Berger, Roger. 'Contemporary Anglophone Literary Theory: The Return of Fanon', *Research in African Literatures*, 21, 1 (Spring 1990) 141-51.

Brydon, Diana. 'New Approaches to the New Literatures in English: Are we in Danger of Incorporating Disparity?' in *A Shaping of Connections: Commonwealth Studies Then and Now*, eds Hena Maes-Jelinek, Kirsten Holst Petersen and Anna Rutherford (Sydney: Dangaroo Press, 1989) 89-99.

Burgess, Anthony. 'Sherlock Holmes and His World', *The Literary Half-Yearly*, 30, 2 (July 1989) 15-23.

Emenyonu, Ernest. 'Who does Flora Nwapa Write For?', *African Literature Today*, 7, Focus on Criticism (1975) 28–37.

Irele, Abiola. 'The Criticism of Modern African Literature', in *Perspectives on African Literature*, ed. Christopher Heywood (London: Heinemann, 1971) 9–30.

Izevbaye, D. S. 'The State of Criticism in African Literature', *African Literature Today*, 7, Focus on Criticism (1975) 1–19.

Lindfors, Bernth. 'The Blind Men and the Elephant', *African Literature Today*, 7, Focus on Criticism (1975) 53–64.

Ogbaa, Kalu. 'African Critics on African Literary Criticism: An Interview with Ben Obumselu'. *The Literary Half-Yearly*, 30, 2 (July 1989) 82–104.

Omoifo, Isi. 'Little Comfort from the Poet-President: Review of Ezenwa-Ohaeto's *I Wan Bi President*', *African Guardian* (14 November 1988) 29.

Saro-Wiwa, Ken. *Sozaboy*. (Port Harcourt: Saros Publishers, 1985).

Schipper, Mineke. (ed.) *Unheard Words: Women and Literature in Africa, the Arab World, Asia, the Caribbean and Latin America*. (London: Allison and Busby, 1985). Translated by Barbara Potter Fasting.

Shaka, Femi. 'Memo on Misrule: Review of Ezenwa-Ohaeto's *I Wan Bi President*', *African Concord*, 4, 22 (30 October 1989) 37.

Tomoloju. Ben. 'So-so Pidgin for Calabar', *The Guardian* (12 May 1989) 11.

Wake, Clive. 'Practical Criticism or Literary Commentary', *Research in African Literatures*, 16, 1 (Spring 1985) 5–19.

Story & Narrative in the Novels of Ayi Kwei Armah

Leif Lorentzon

Readers of Ayi Kwei Armah's five novels invariably agree they are novels of great diversity. It is particularly between the first three and the last two where the change is most noticeable. One critic even goes so far as to talk about the early and the late Armah.[1] When other critics more acutely instead stress the homogeneity between the five novels, it is predominantly theme and imagery that is considered. Yet most readers would insist that the novels are remarkably dissimilar for a single author's works. I believe this largely has to do with a change of narrative strategy.

Narratology is the discipline with which we can study this change of narrative posture. With its roots in Russian formalism early this century, it was further developed and introduced to a larger audience during the seventies in France. Today, American universities are perhaps most productive on the subject. It is in other words a decidedly Western theoretical approach. This should not of course stop students of African literature from making full use of these theories. As in any science, the scholar of literature must under no circumstances discard theories before examining them. It would be uncommonly daft not to test the validity of narratology on the modern African novel, since the novel is the genre which essentially generated the theory. And just as the theory in this case is Western, so is the genre, the novel: 'the only literary art form which has been totally imported' to Africa.[2] I am certainly not suggesting a disregard for African poetics. But 'there is no African society that, to my [Abiola Irele's] knowledge, has carried the judgement of texts and reflection upon literature to the same degree of

53

elaboration which we are today used to in the Western tradition.'[3] There is no better practice than narratology when we are (which we are) interested in the narrative strategies of narrative texts.

Structural narratology, which is what is considered here, has been accused of only revealing the already obvious: 'The few models that survived ... became so second-nature as to make their very use in detailed analysis almost unnecessary, their codes and categories leaping to the naked eye in a sad, professional deformation of reading for pleasure.'[4] If this judgement applies to some aspects of narratology, it is absolutely the position of this essay that a narrative close-reading of a novel reveals phenomena in a text which can be put into a larger literary or social context. It is a matter of 'mobilizing narratological insights for other objects'.[5] It may, for instance, be possible to recognise something of the supposedly progressive Africanisation of Armah's prose, by initially analysing the narrative strategy of the novels and then putting the result of each analysis into a larger perspective of the genre and African narratives of all kinds.

This essay will refer to results of a close reading of Armah's novels on a macro- rather than a micro-level, in which the theories of Gérard Genette, inter alia, have been used. A complete analysis according to Genette's model will indeed attend to some that are obvious on a first reading, but it also reveals features which are significant for a comparison with other literatures. It is some of these aspects that I wish to pay attention to here.

Genette's method essentially considers relationship between *story*, the narrative events, and *narrative*, the discourse that narrates these events.[6] Of great interest then is the discrepancy between the order of the events in the story, and their order of appearance in the discourse. One of the distinctions of a narrative is that it, alone of all texts, has two time-orders. Rarely are the events of a story in narrative texts told in the order they occur in the story. Genette defines as *anachrony* 'the various types of discordance between the two orderings of story and narrative.'[7] A retrospective temporal movement he calls *analepsis* and the forward one *prolepsis*, in relation to the *primary story-time* of the narrative.[8] Analepsis is by far the more common anachrony in narratives of all kinds and so also in Armah's novels, where prolepsis appears only parenthetically.

If we compare the analepses of Armah's five novels, we will find that *Two Thousand Seasons* has no analepses while the other novels are full of them. In *The Beautyful Ones Are Not Yet Born* and *The Healers* the retrospective temporal anachronies stretch beyond the commencement of the primary story-time (*external*), while in *Fragments* and *Why Are We So Blest?* the analepses essentially remain within that temporal zone (*internal*). When Teacher in *The Beautyful Ones* remembers times before liberation he does so outside the scope of the primary story-time of the novel. The anachronies of *The Healers* are also dominated by external analepses, and just as in *The Beautyful Ones* they are huddled together in one part of the novel. Here it is Densu remembering the first time he met the healer Damfo, Araba Jesiwa and his sweetheart Ajoa during his walk through the forest. In both these novels analepsis is conventionally used to give, for the story, essential background information from outside the primary story-time.

Fragments and *Why Are We So Blest?*, however, are dominated by internal analepsis. The Outdooring is one example of an event in the former that is told much later in the narrative, in relation to when it happens in the story. And *Why Are We So Blest?* is a virtual temporal jigsaw puzzle. This kind of narrative, where the temporal order of the primary story-time is internally distorted, appears first with the modern novel after *Madame Bovary* and particularly with William Faulkner and the French *nouveau roman*. 'With the coming of the twentieth century, plotting in narrative became dominated by time ... plots began to be developed which were based on re-arranging time.'[9] So if external analepsis is conventional and internal modern, we find that Armah's first and last novels in this respect are traditionally narrated, while *Fragments* and *Why Are We So Blest?* are in a modernistic tradition.

This should perhaps not mislead us to be too conclusive regarding the Africanness of these novels. Walter J. Ong claims that linear plot is incompatible with the oral tale, and recent speech-act theory insists that 'conversational narratives and literary narratives share essentially the same characteristics'.[10] An oral narrator, however, would never tell a tale as anachronistically as we read them in *Why Are We So Blest?* and Faulkner's *Absalom, Absalom!*, where even the reader struggles with temporal entanglements. The listener, and I dare say even the raconteur, would be utterly lost. And when contemporary African writers recreate indigenous epics they narrate chronologically, if not linearly or for the novel conventionally, which Mazisi Kunene's epics, as well as Armah's last two novels, bear witness to.

To further investigate the rhythm of a narrative it is essential to compare story-time with page-space, or what Genette calls the *pseudo-time* of the reading. What is considered then is the speed of the narrative. He distinguishes between four narrative movements: *pause, scene, summary* and *ellipsis*. In pause the narrative halts, to either describe the space of the story, the diegesis, or reflect upon it without any story-time passing. Genette does not make this distinction between the two qualities of pause, as the result regarding the speed of the narrative is the same, it pauses. Yet I believe we can discover a significant aspect if we differentiate between a descriptive and a reflective pause in novels in general, and in the novels of Armah in particular.

The Beautyful Ones is the only novel of his which is generous with descriptive pause. It is during the first day of the story we find famous passages like this:

> The banister had originally been a wooden one, and to this time it was possible to see, in the deepest of the cracks between the swellings of other matter, a dubious piece of deeply aged brown wood. And there were many cracks, though most of them did not reach all the way down to the wood underneath.[11]

No story-time passes here in a passage which describes story-space, diegesis. And its symbolic significance links it to an allegorical modern tradition of *Moby Dick* and *The Trial*.

If we add descriptive pause to all the slow summaries, which only this of Armah's novels exhibits, we realise that the speed of this novel is slow, at least in parts. In a summary, story-time passes with various speeds. We find very fast summary in *Two Thousand Seasons*, for instance, when 20 kings and their reigns are accounted for in a few pages.[12] In *The Beautyful Ones* there is slow summary:

The driver climbed down onto the road from his seat, took a crumpled packet of Tuskers from his shirt pocket, stuck a bent cigarette in his mouth, and lit a match. The head refused to catch, however; there was only the humid orange glow as the driver resignedly threw away the stick and took out another. (p. 1)

Slow summary and descriptive pause of this kind is found in plenty of prose, but in excess only in the *nouveau roman* of an Alain Robbe-Grillet text.

Armah's first novel is also abundant with reflective pause:

The wood underneath would win and win till the end of time ... Of course it was in the nature of the wood to rot with age. The polish, it was supposed, would catch the rot. But of course in the end it was the rot which imprisoned everything in its effortless embrace. It did not really have to fight. Being was enough. (p. 12)

No story-time passes when the narrator, as close to the protagonist as in *Fragments*, reflects upon the diegesis. In *Why Are We So Blest?* it is the characters themselves who meditate in their notebooks. While *The Beautyful Ones* is the only one of Armah's novels that is comparably rich in descriptive pause, the first three novels are all rich in reflective pause. *Why Are We So Blest?* is extreme in this regard, as the whole novel can be understood as a reflective pause; it is certainly the dominant narrative movement. This would ally these introspective characters with modern literary figures as Raskolnikov and Stephen Daedalus, and such an existential hero as Antoine Roquentin. In Armah's later histories there is little if any reflective pause. Consequently the heroes are more types than characters with diverse qualities. These two novels are instead typical of that 'connective tissue par excellence of novelistic narrative, whose fundamental rhythm is defined by the alteration of summary and scene'.[13]

Later Genette expanded with a fifth narrative movement, *reflexive digression*, which accounts for something essential in oral narrating and found in Armah's last two novels.[14] The reflective pause reflects inside the story (*intradiegetic*), whereas the reflexive digression is a digression from that story, a reflection outside it (*extra-diegetic*). But it does not have to be an oral phenomenon. This kind of digression is certainly found in *Tristam Shandy* and *Jacques le fataliste*, to mention two earlier novels where the reflexive digression seems to dominate the monumentally authorial narration. It is also abundant in the post-modernist novel, where the narrator, or rather the fictionalised author 'is free, once again to break in upon the fictional world' from another ontological level.[15]

In Armah's last two novels the narrator intrusions are, however, decidedly of an oral nature:

> Ah, Fasseke, words fail the storyteller. Fasseke Belen Tigui, master of masters in the art of eloquence, lend me strength. Send me eloquence to finish what I have begun . . . Send me words Mokopu Mofolo. Send me words of eloquence. Words are mere wind, but wind too has always been part of our work, this work of sowers for the future, the work of the storyteller.[16]

Narrator intrusion of this nature is found in oral literature and that written close to it. The Homeric invocation of the muse is an early example of this kind of meta-narrative, narrative about the narrating, in Western literature. In traditional African tales we find it, for instance, in D. T. Niane's version of *Sundiata* and J. P. Clark's *The Ozidi Saga*.[17]

There is another kind of reflexive digression of a meta-narrative character found both in African traditional orature, like *The Ozidi Saga*, and Armah's last two novels. I am here thinking of the narrator's rhetorical questions to the reader. In *Two Thousand Seasons* there is much of this: 'Dovi had suffered, but who is it saying any of us have been alone in our suffering?' (p. 180). The story pauses here, but with Genette's terminology we can best define it as reflexive digression of a quality found amply in traditional African orature. Ruth Finnegan attests to this in her monumental book, and in W. M. Kabira's study of East African orature we are shown how one raconteur uses the audience 'by asking rhetorical questions and making the audience fill in gaps in her story'.[18] A tentative proposal would suggest that the occurrence of different kinds of pause in Armah's novels, links the latter two histories with the oral narrative and the earlier three with the modern novel.

Of the other narrative movements we shall briefly look at ellipsis, where story-time is unaccounted for. Genette distinguishes between the *explicit*, when the ellipsis is indicated in the text, and the *implicit*, when the reader must deduce the ellipsis from a lacuna of story-time in the narrative.

The former is a common narrative figure: 'When [many] days had passed that his wives had remained pregnant, one day six of his wives pulled through; they gave birth merely to female children.'[19] Here the explicit ellipsis functions as a strengthening adhesive. The opposite is the case when the implicit ellipsis rather breaks the continuum of story-time without indicating this in the discourse. This is the case in such novels as *Light in August* and *La route des Flandres*. In Armah's first two novels the implicit ellipses dominate. They are also indefinite in that they do not indicate the time ellipsed. In *Why Are We So Blest?* ellipses are explicit due to the notebook technique, and thanks to the occasional date also sometimes definite. As the narrative rarely in itself, however, reveals the ellipses, it is possible to regard this novel, too, as dominated by implicit narrating.

This is certainly not the case with his last two novels. *Two Thousand Seasons* has the greatest time span, which demands either very fast summary or ellipsis. There is plenty of both. The ellipses are always explicit and often definite: 'A hundred seasons we spent in this slow flowering.' (p. 50). Even if temporally shorter than in *Two Thousand Seasons* the ellipses are of the same quality in *The Healers*. The narrating of the games in the first two parts is typical: 'The last day, Saturday, came, the day when the champion for the entire games would be chosen.' (p. 42)

The generalisation regarding the modernistic and conventional nature of implicit and explicit ellipsis, is just that, a generalisation. Yet it indicates one specific reason why readers find Armah's early novels modernistic and *Two Thousand Seasons* and *The Healers* closer to African traditional narratives.

Genette discusses the distance between the story and the narrative in terms of narrative of events and speech. I shall disregard both of these and instead observe the narrating of thoughts. For this we have to leave Genette's otherwise so elaborate model, as he does not acknowledge a narrating of consciousness, and turn to Dorrit Cohn in order to properly account for passages such as this from *The Beautyful Ones*:

> The allocation clerk is in there with his boss for something like half an hour, and when they emerge he is closely followed by the super-visor and they are both smiling broad, very satisfied smiles. Let them

> smile. This place is kind to them, so let them smile. In another country
> they would be in jail. Here they are heroes. (pp. 128-9)

The last three sentences seem to come directly from the consciousness of 'the man'. Cohn calls this *narrated monologue*,
when in a third-person context there is a reflection, as if in first
person, from one of the story's characters.[20] Jane Austen is
generally considered as the author who first successfully and
extensively used this technique, which later was perfected by
Gustave Flaubert. Ever since then it has become the most common
method for presenting character's thoughts in a third-person
context.

The Beautyful Ones and *Fragments* are dominated by narrated
monologue. Both novels are predominantly third-person narratives
with a narrator extremely close to the protagonists. Naana's
chapters in *Fragments*, however, are of a different quality. With
the exception of her account of Baako's departure in the first
chapter (*self-narration*), her chapters are best understood as
autonomous monologue, which is 'by definition, a discourse
addressed to no one, a gratuitous verbal agitation without a
communicative aim'.[21] This is a good characterisation of Naana's
narrative:

> From the world and the life around me, nothing comes to me. My eyes
> are no longer windows through the wall of my flesh but a part of this
> blinding skin itself. Soon my ears too will be shut, and my soul within
> my body will be closed up, completely alone.[22]

Even if not as radical as the Penelope chapter in *Ulysses*, it clearly
belongs to the tradition of the modern novel. With yet another
tentative generalisation this would suggest that Armah's first two
novels, in their narrating of thoughts, are modern.

Armah's following novel is completely dominated by self-
narration in its conventional notebook technique, which links
it, both in form and introspective probing, with a tradition of
epistolary and diary novels like *Malte Laurids Brigge* and *La
Nausée*. Except for the narrator's peculiar plural self-narration,
there is not much thought narrating in either *Two Thousand
Season* or in *The Healers*. The little there is in the latter is in
psycho-narration, when the narrator tells the reader what the
character thinks: 'He thought of the coming year he would have
to spend at Esuano and tried to imagine it as time usefully spent.'

(p. 105). Ever since writers dared to explore the mind of their characters, this has been the most common technique used in doing it. It is also the kind found in African traditional tales, as well as in old epics such as *Gilgamesh* and *Beowulf*. So while Armah's first three novels in their narrating of consciousness resemble the modern novel, his latter two are traditional bordering on oral form.

The concept which has attracted more commentary than any of Genette's innovations, is that of the *focalisation* of the narrative. He separates the notion of point-of-view into *mood*: through which character is the narrative perceived? who sees it? and *voice*: who is the narrator? who speaks? I shall for lack of space not consider voice here, but instead end the essay with a quick comparative glance at the mood of Armah's novels.

Genette differentiates between three kinds of perspectives he calls *non-internal-* and *external-focalisation*. *Two Thousand Seasons* is the only Armah novel with unshakable non-focalisation. Its narrator knows and says more than any character in the story, which is the most conventional perspective of traditional tales. *The Healers* at first seems to be internally focalised through Densu, but there are passages where the narrator leaves Densu, and reveals a non-focalised perspective. And the narrator is quite explicit about it: 'He [Asamoa Nkwanta] now searched the lines for signs of Densu, but could see no sign of him.' (p. 286). Densu soon appears, but he has then been absent from the narrative for some ten pages.

In his first three novels Armah uses internal focalisation. In *The Beautyful Ones* it is chiefly fixed to 'the man', with the exception of the first few pages and Teacher's narrative. *Fragments* and *Why Are We So Blest?* are both variably internal. With each chapter in the first and each notebook entry in the latter, the perspective of the narrative changes. While non-focalisation is typical of the oral tale and traditional novels like *Le Père Goriot* and *Things Fall Apart*, the variable internal is found in many since *Madame Bovary*, and characteristic of many novels we consider archetypes of the modernistic novel: *To the Lighthouse* and *The Sound and Fury*. So this is yet another narrative reason why readers and critics have found Armah's first three novels more modern than the later histories.

Ever since Derek Wright's brilliant book on Armah's Africanness readers have had to reconsider their initial impression of Armah's fiction. Here Wright unearthed African subtexts in precisely those novels that had been considered modern and Western, and discarded the later histories as 'mannered experimentation with simulated orality . . . and simplistic historical vision'.[23] My view here is rather methodological. A structural narrative reading complements an analysis such as his, where the text is put into a specific context. With a narratological approach it is possible to isolate certain features of a narrative and study these in a comparative light, and, if we want (which we do) place the result into the larger perspective of the whole genre.

It is this I have tried to indicate here; or rather to illustrate how useful a narratological analysis can be to an understanding of a writer's oeuvre. By way of close reading we realise how Ayi Kwei Armah's five novels are narratively structured. We compare them with one another, and then, rather presumptuously perhaps, with all the narratives of the world. This has, of course, only been suggested here. I nevertheless hope that I have managed to imply the value of at least these theories and methods in the study of the modern African novel. It would indeed be sad if we were to deny ourselves the pleasure of testing the rewards of modern theoretical thinking on African literary tales. There is possibly something here for everyone, including students of African literature, a literature which 'is an amalgamation, a syncretism of past and present'.[24] It deserve the some tools or methods of criticism as other literatures.

NOTES

1. Simon Gikandi, *Reading the African Novel* (London: James Currey, 1987) 73.
2. Dennis Dathorne, *The Invisible Present* (New York: Harper & Row 1975) 53. See also note 6 below regarding what was literally imported to Africa with the colonists.
3. Abiola Irele, *The African Experience in Literature and Ideology* (London: Heinemann, 1981) 18.
4. Christine Brooke-Rose, 'Whatever Happened to Narratology?', *Poetics Today*, 11, 2 (Summer 1990) 287.

5. Mieke Bal, 'The Point of Narratology', *Poetics Today*, 11, 4 (1990) 730. The interested reader may turn to this and the following two issues of *Poetics Today* for a valuable orientation of the present status of narratology: 11, 2 (1990); 12, 3 (1991).

6. Gérard Genette, *Narrative Discourse* (Oxford: Basil Blackwell, 1980) 27. It is a section, 'Discours du récit', of *Figures III* (Paris: Editions du Seuil, 1972). Genette's distinction makes the obvious apparent; it was the novel as *discourse* which was imported to Africa, while the story, of course, has been present for thousands of years.

7. Genette, 36.

8. Genette calls the temporal level to which all anachronies are defined *the first narrative*, Genette, 48. But as that well can be confused with the first narrative in a discourse, as in *The Beautyful Ones Are Not Yet Born*, where there is more than one narrative, I find Bal's term more suitable. See Mieke Bal, *Narratology* (Toronto: University of Toronto Press, 1985) 57. Originally in Dutch: *De theorie van vertellen en verhalen* (Muiderberg: Coutinho, 1980).

9. Robert Scholes and Robert Kellog, *The Nature of Narrative* (New York: Oxford University Press) 235.

10. Joyce Tolliver, 'Discourse Analysis and the Interpretation of Literary Narrative', *Style*, 24, 2, 266; and Walter J. Ong, *Orality and Literacy* (London: Routledge, 1988 [1982], chapter 6, but particularly p. 145.

11. Ayi Kwei Armah, *The Beautyful Ones Are Not Yet Born* (London: Heinemann, 1968) p. 12 of the reset edition of 1975.

12. Ayi Kwei Armah, *Two Thousand Seasons* (London: Heinemann, 1979) 63–6.

13. Genette, 97.

14. Gérard Genette, *Narrative Discourse Revisited* (Ithaca: New York, and Cornell University Press, 1988) 36–7. Originally in the French: *Nouveau discours du récit* (Paris: Editions du Seuil, 1983).

15. Brian McHale, *Postmodernist Fiction* (New York and London: Methuen, 1987) 199.

16. Ayi Kwei Armah, *The Healers* (London: Heinemann, 1979) 63.

17. See D. T. Niane, *Sundiata* (Harlow: Longman, 1965) 40–41; and J. P. Clark, *The Ozidi Saga* (Ibadan: Ibadan University Press, 1977) 321 and 326.

18. Ruth Finnegan, *Oral Literature in Africa* (London and New York: Oxford University Press, 1970) 385.

19. Daniel Biebuyck, ed. &. trans., *The Mwindo Epic* (Los Angeles: University of California Press, 1969) 53.

20 Dorrit Cohn, *Transparent Minds* (Princeton: Princeton University Press, 1978) 13. For a discussion of this particular technique of third-person thought narrating, which in English for long has been neglected, see also Brian McHale, 'Free Indirect Discourse: A Survey of Recent Accounts', *PTL: Journal for Descriptive Poetics and Theory of Literature*, 3, 2 (April 1978).

21. Cohn, 225.

22. Ayi Kwei Armah, *Fragments* (London: Heinemann, 1974) 278.

23. Derek Wright, *Ayi Kwei Armah's Africa* (London: Hans Zell, 1989) viii.

24. Solomon O. Iyasere, 'Cultural Formalism and Criticism of Modern African Literature', *Journal of Modern African Studies*, 14, 2 (1976) 328.

Multiple Witnesses, Multiple Stories: Subversion of the Story-telling-Interpretation Processes in Court Trials

Emmanuel Yewah

Prefatory Note

I must admit my own difficulty in isolating one critical method from a myriad of contemporary critical approaches that I have naturalised and which have become an integral part of my theoretical knowledge and therefore find themselves interwoven into my discursive system. So my theoretical approach in the article that follows is rather eclectic in that it draws from many theoretical bases with a bias towards textual analysis, traditionalist aesthetics, and deconstruction.

In a 1987 interview, Jacques Derrida explains that *décon-struction* used as a French word, 'means not "destroying" but "undoing", while analysing the different layers of a structure to know how it has been built.' Everything which is not natural, he continues, 'has a structure, and has been built; and deconstruction is, to some extent, a way of analysing the structure . . .' (p. 2). Indeed my reading of *Le Procès d'un Prix Nobel* by Séraphin Ndaot and Patrick Ilboudo's *Le Procès du muet* as a subversion of the story-telling-interpretation processes is an attempt to undo the structure of the received tradition in the law. On the one hand, subversion takes the form of introducing into the judging process a multiplicity of character witnesses and, on the other, the silence of the accused during their own trial becomes a strategy of subversion.

Le Procès d'un Prix Nobel uses the multiplicity of witnesses, each telling his own story, as a vehicle to introduce into the judging process such elements as politics, society, economics, and religion that have been repressed by a rule-oriented legal system bent on preserving its autonomy. In so doing, the text, not only breaks down the constraints imposed by the rules of evidence but, in the words of Sanford Levinson and Steven Mailloux, 'challenge[s] the established boundaries and disciplinary demarcations' (p. xi).

By breaking down the evidentiary restrictions and prohibitions as such, the text manages to 'deconstruct' the legal structure, thereby providing those witnesses with the freedom to turn a rule-centred courtroom into a lieu of 'free play'. In such a space in which witnesses think and express themselves freely, the focus is no longer on rigid formal rules of evidence that have always been used as a pretext to leave certain issues and questions out of discourses in the courtroom, but rather on those other aspects as personal stories, commentaries on society, and the role of the ancestral spirit in the judging process and in reinstituting equilibrium in society. John Conley and William O'Barr have observed similar procedures of litigants telling their stories in an unrestricted manner and their attempts to use everyday discourse rules in the courtroom in what they have called 'the informal courts' in American society. Such unrestricted narratives by litigants and their witnesses, in this case character witnesses, are also reminiscent of court procedures in some traditional African societies. In courtroom situations in those societies, truth was not determined through a carefully coded system but through heated discussions, exchanges between the plaintiff and the accused or their witnesses. As Jonathan Egbor, one of the accused in T. M. Aluko's *Wrong Ones in the Dock*, frustrated with the imported 'truth-inhibiting judicial system' puts it, '[I] did not see the sense in a legal system in which a witness who tells a lie is allowed to go unchallenged immediately, while the lie is still hot' (p. 164).

Undoing or laying bare of the legal structure through the silence of the accused in *Le Procès du muet*, helps to bring into the process a dimension left out due to constraints imposed by the rules of evidence, that is, the spiritual as represented by the ancestor. By bringing into the discourse the ancestor, as the physically absent yet spiritually omnipresent, as the one who is assumed to know the truth as it relates to specific cultures, my appeal here, as in the case above, is to traditional aesthetics. In that case the silence of the accused becomes a way of conjuring the presence of the ancestor to render judgement in a process whose end would otherwise have been permanently deferred. The silence undermines the judge's training in a received legal system which has built-in rules related to silence. The judge is therefore rendered powerless. That powerless space helps to open the way, which, in turn, makes it possible for the intervention of the ancestor, whom, as I assert later, is the real judge.

Richard Posner has stated in one of his studies of law and literature that 'both legal and literary scholarship are centrally concerned with the meaning of texts ... And legal scholarship, like literary scholarship, consists to a significant extent of commentary on texts ...' (p. 8). As such, the study that follows, interdisciplinary and eclectic in its approach, relies on close textual analysis of two literary works to show how textual elements are used to undo the imported legal tradition and in the process resurrect the repressed elements or those issues and questions that have been left out of legal discourses due to restrictions imposed by rules of law.

Un mutisme est plus sage et plus digne. (Silence is wiser and more dignified)

Le silence pour nous n'est pas une marque de sagesse, ni de dignité. Devant la cour ne se taisent que ceux qui ont quelque chose à se reprocher.

(Silence for us is neither a sign of wisdom nor of dignity. Only those who have something to hide maintain silence in their own trial.)

Stories are among our most basic units of communication; they permit us to translate our impressions of a distant event into a form that will allow the listener in an immediate situation to grasp its significance. The story form also aids the listener in drawing certain conclusions about the interpretation ...
(Bennett, 'Storytelling in Criminal Trials')

Introduction

The sign 'Silence: Court in Session' around court houses in some African countries reflects both the serious and the solemn nature of the court and the kind of atmosphere of awe that surrounds it. It also points to the fact that silence helps to create a serene atmosphere conducive to the search for what may be accepted as truth or truths by the litigants in a trial. Some defendants in trials in courts of law and in works of fiction, however, have interpreted the sign literally to mean that they have to maintain silence or 'take the fifth', as Americans would say, even in their own trial. As such, they have used the sign as a defence strategy to subvert the judging-interpretation processes as in *Le Procès du muet*. *Le Procès d'un Prix Nobel* subverts the process by introducing a multiplicity of witnesses each telling a story irrelevant to the main story. Using both texts as sources of reference, this work seeks to show 1) the centrality of story-telling in trials, 2) the use of stories in the judging process, and 3) the idea that trials in these works as in many other literary works often serve as a metaphor for something else. Moreover, the question might be asked as to why the texts engage in the subversive enterprise or indeed what is the point of subverting the story-telling process. One might argue that it is an attempt to question, indeed to demystify commonly held assumptions about the nature of truth and/or justice. Because subversion either through silence or irrelevance defers resolution permanently, it will be shown that any semblance of resolution at the end of both texts is attributable to a spiritual or ancestral intervention.

The subversive use of silence and multiple judges

In *Le Procès du muet*, Pass Yam and Biga Zansoiba, the main characters are brought to trial accused of having embezzled the funds of a multinational corporation. But on the advice of their counsels, they have decided to maintain silence. In such a case in which the accused have opted for silence or in the words of the judge '*ont choisi . . . d'être aphones*' (have chosen to be aphonic) or '*ont perdu l'usage de la parole,*' (have lost their speaking abilities) (p. 112), the question is, how does the presiding judge go about making his decision? In other words, on what does the judge base his/her judgement when such criminals have refused to produce stories that will aid the court and its audience 'in drawing certain conclusions about interpretation'? For as Lance Bennett has pointed out, story-telling by litigants and other participants plays a very important role in criminal trials. As he writes, 'stories are among our most basic units of communication . . .' Stories, he adds, 'are powerful means of transmitting precise interpretations of distant and complex events to people who either did not witness those events or who did not grasp them from the story-teller's perspective' (p. 3).

Moreover, the silence of the accused seems to create room or a stage for the same trial taking place in the courtroom to be carried out simultaneously in the minds of the accused. The question then becomes who is the 'real' judge? Given that in some African traditional societies it is believed that a criminal's conscience is his/her most critical judge, is one to conclude that the judge in this case is the conscience of the accused (if at all they have a conscience)? As Pius Nkashama has noted, conscience plays a very important role in the judging process in many African societies: '*Les sociétés africaines dans leurs traditions anciennes,*' he writes, '*avaient institué des règles de dénonciation, qui obligeaient tout individu à "interroger sa conscience"* ' (p. 201).[1] The importance of conscience is also stressed by someone in the court audience who remarks when Biga Zansoiba breaks down in tears that '*il n'a qu'à parler pour libérer son âme. Seule la vérité peut le mettre en paix avec sa conscience*' (p. 110).[2] If silence helps to highlight the nature of conscience, if conscience is so conceived as judge and jury, then the silence of the accused is in itself another form of story-telling. But it is a story that does not lend itself to interpretation by the court since it takes place in the mind.

Textual evidence also suggests that in the state of silence of the defendants the trial is raised to the spiritual level. In this case could one conclude that it is the spirits of the ancestors, working as they do, in silence, that become the real judges? But given that various parts of the text dealing with the trial are in quotations and are written in the form of anonymous court reports, newspaper clippings, which the narrator is reading and translating to his elderly uncle for the latter's interpretation, one can also conclude that the real judges are the narrator and his uncle. One should not forget to add to this list of possible judges 'la présidente' or the presiding judge even though she does not seem to have the legal power and the authority or the 'judicially articulated levels of proof or internally refined bodies of legal doctrine' (p. 38) to force the accused to break their silence and tell stories. Such stories will help the judge, in the words of Lawrence Rosen, 'in reasoning her way to a final decision' (p. 4). The text uses silence and this multiplicity of possible judges to subvert the judging process.

Besides this subversion, there seem to be two different trials going on simultaneously or, as suggested above, the same trial seems to be taking place at different levels such that one can talk of other trials within the main trial. For instance, at the end of the main trial one of the accused is found guilty and sentenced to fourteen years hard labour and the restitution of the money stolen. As the decision is being read for the second accused, however, there is, to use a theatre metaphor, a dimming of lights on stage and by the time the lights come on again, the audience is transported to a scene in which the father of the narrator, who had not been in court, is being taken directly to prison by the police. He is accused of misappropriating the funds of a regional corporation. One wonders, especially based on the narrator's comments after his father's arrest, if he had not been imagining or staging, in his mind, his own father's silent trial throughout his reading of the court report. The exact correspondence between the verdict of the trial and the arrest of the narrator's father seems to suggest that the two accused and the narrator's father are one and the same person. In that case and as mentioned above, the text has created this simulacrum of multiplicity of interpretive subjects and situations to foil the story-telling process.

As stated earlier, the defendants have been advised by their attorneys to maintain silence as a way to question the jurisdiction of the court of Tenkotenga (the fictional country in which the trial takes place) over such a case with international dimensions. Underlying the advice of the counsels is the very pertinent question of whether the legal system of Tenkotenga, or for that matter the legal system of one country, is competent to try and convict in such an international crime (given that the judge herself is not quoting or drawing from any body of laws). It is possible that the treaty law that binds the members of the international organisation does empower individual countries to try such criminals and convict them. Unfortunately the judge does not cite such a law. Raising the question of jurisdiction of the court of Tenkotenga does not mean that the counsels would rather have the case tried by an international court, but they are suggesting rather shrewdly and subversively that it be purely and simply thrown out of court for reason of incompetence. As one of the defence attorneys declares, 'je redis que votre tribunal doit réfléchir dans la sérénité la plus absolue et se déclarer incompétent pour juger cette affaire' (p. 81).[3]

Faced with the silence of the defendants and the attempt by the defence counsels to undermine the jurisdiction of her court, and therefore, of her own legal power, the judge develops strategies to force the defendants to talk, even if what they say might not be directly related to the case for which they are being tried. For instance, rather than talking tough, she makes statements that appeal to their conscience: 'vous avez le devoir de rendre compte aujourd'hui aux peuples de l'Union, ceux qui vous avaient mandaté pour agir en leur nom pour leurs intérêts . . . Vous devez être un homme responsable jusqu'au bout' (pp. 38–9).[4] She makes statements that reinforce the multiplicity of titles that the defendants have accumulated, the kind of pseudo-image of the untouchables that they have created for themselves. She asks general questions not directly related to the case, but questions that sollicit their 'highly respected' and 'infinitely valuable' opinions: 'vous êtes un très haut cadre africain, vous êtes président fondateur du Club des Amis des pays sahéliens, vous êtes économiste. Vous avez été ancien ministre du plan et du développement de Djandjan. Pouvez-vous nous donner votre conception du développement de l'Afrique?' (p. 106)[5]

When both attempts fail to force the accused to talk, the judge changes her strategy. Instead of appealing to their conscience and their egos, she makes derogatory remarks about them, accusing them among other things of having invested the money they embezzled in drug trafficking, of suffering from financial bulimia. She calls them prototypes of rotten civil servants, the rubbish of African societies, dangerous beasts. She condemns them in these harsh terms:

Les accusés ici présents sont les ordures de nos sociétés africaines, des bêtes dangereuses qui ont occasionné des dégats dans leurs divagations . . . peut-être Monsieur Pass Yam a-t-il placé l'argent dans la drogue. Ministre, il a été compromis dans un trafic illicite de diamant . . . Les deux prévenus sont les prototypes même de fonction-naires pourris . . . Monsieur Biga Zansoiba, vous êtes un corps malade, vous êtes atteint de la boulimie financière. Vous êtes un délinquant . . . Quant à vous Monsieur Pass Yam, vous êtes un oiseau rare. Disons même que vous êtes chargé de tous les péchés . . . (p. 109ff.)[6]

All these are attempts to incite them into reacting verbally.

The silence of the defendants, subversive as it is, might simply be a reflection of the fact that corruption and embezzlement of public funds, rampant though they may be, are nevertheless such imperceptible acts when they are being done that they cannot really be expressed in a spoken language. Given the status of the two accused in their society, their refusal to speak might be a way of undermining the authority of the presiding judge who happens to be a woman. Moreover, as two high officials who are now estranged from their society, their silence might be a cynical commentary on a legal system that protects and perpetuates the illegal political institutions that they have exploited for so long but that has finally caught up with them.

The nature of truth and/or justice

If *Le Procès du muet* uses silence and the multiplicity of possible judges, interpretive subjects and situations to subvert the judging process, in *Le Procès d'un Prix Nobel*, subversion takes the form of introducing into the process a plethora of witnesses, each giving a fragmentary, incomplete, inconsistent account or story with no apparent connection to the case in point. In subverting the story-telling process through irrelevance, this text seeks to show the difficulty, indeed the impossibility of knowing the truth. More importantly, it seeks to question the nature of truth. Is there such a thing as Truth or multiple truths? (The use of capital 'T' is to underscore the fact that the reference here is to the Idea of truth). One of the defence attorneys has argued that there is no such thing as a single Truth but rather a multiplicity of truths: '*il n'existe pas une Vérité, il y a des vérités; chacun détient et expose sa vérité. Entre la vérité psychique et la vérité matérielle, il y a une vérité fondament . . .* (p. 87).[7]

If there is not a single immanent Truth, the basic question in this text, as in the one discussed earlier is, can justice be achieved based on multiple irrelevant stories? Can the court effectively carry out its legal duties, when the courtroom itself, a lieu par excellence to produce serious legal stories, has been turned into a stage for what Richard Posner calls a 'dramatic confrontation between rational methods of inquiry and the non-rational side of human nature' (p. 354) that is, when the courtroom has become a stage for a dramatic presentation of a farce in which the actors or multiple witnesses produce multiple stories? Can the court synthesise these disparate and incomplete truths to a version of truth acceptable to all the parties in the trial?

Peter Goodrich has stated that 'legal discourse is ... concerned with truth' or in the words of one of the defence attorneys '*la mission de l'avocat n'est-elle pas . . . de rechercher fébrilement la vérité . . .?*' (p. 87)[8] Posner would add that both law and literature are 'centrally concerned with the meaning[s] of texts' (p. 8). To discover such truth(s) or actually to establish a system of meanings, however, it is absolutely imperative that there be no discrepancies between the defendants' stories (and the various interpretive possibilities to which they lend themselves) and those of other participants in the trial i.e., their respective witnesses.

It should be pointed out that *Le Procès d'un Prix Nobel* is not teleological, that is, it is not so much concerned with the verdict of the trial as with the processes which involve both story-telling and the interpretations of those stories. But at the same time, and as indicated earlier, the defence counsels systematically subvert these processes by introducing a multiplicity of witnesses from diverse backgrounds and by constantly interrupting those witnesses so that they do not and cannot tell a coherent and complete story.

Such a subversion of the story-telling process raises the very pertinent question of interpretation, which is central to both literary and legal scholarships, and is also an important operation in the search for truth(s) or meaning(s). Interpretation, Posner writes, 'consists to a significant extent of commentary on texts temporally and culturally remote from the commentator' (p. 8) or in the words of Gregory Leyh, '. . . textual interpretations are always reconstructions of the past, in the light of contemporary practices, interests, and problems' (p. 855). In the process of such reconstructions of the past, story-telling becomes a very important means of translating and transmitting understanding among the participants in the trial and the audience.

In this context, the following comment by Bennett is quite apt. He does not focus on the text per se but on the stories of the litigants. A story, he writes, 'is a reconstruction of an event in the light of the teller's initial perception and immediate judgements about the audience, the interests that appear to be at stake, and, perhaps most importantly, what has gone on before in the situation in which the story is presented' (p. 20).

In his essay referred to earlier Bennett has noted that stories organise information in ways that help the listener to perform three interpretive operations:

> First, the interpreter must be able to locate the central action, the key behavior around which the point of the story will be drawn. Second, the interpreter must construct inferences about the relationships among the surrounding elements in the story that impinge on the central action. The connections among the cast of supporting symbols literally creates the interpretive context for the action or behavior at the center of the story. Finally, the network of symbolic connections drawn around the central action in the story must be tested for internal consistency and descriptive adequacy and completeness. (p. 5)

While the three cognitive operations do indeed provide the ideal interpretive situation, the texts under discussion here create what seem to be central stories or actions but at the same time they systematically subvert, frustrate, any attempts to effect both the second and the third operations that Bennett has identified above. For example in the case of corruption and misappropriation of the funds of an international corporation, the accused refuse to tell their stories; they refuse to use the spoken language which would have helped to define and assess facts about the case.

Multiple witnesses as a subversive strategy

In my second example, Dr Seller, an expatriate from a former colonial power, a religious man, a renowned musician, a medical doctor, and a Nobel laureate for peace, is charged with using his African patients as subjects in his medical research. He is accused of having 'depuis un temps non prescrit, administré à ses malades des substances qui ne convenaient pas, en tout cas peu recommandées par la science médicale. Il lui est également fait grief de s'être livrés à des expériences sur ses patients, lesquelles expériences ont entraîné la mort de ces derniers' (p. 13).[9]

The fact that the statement of accusation is in the passive with no identifiable agent raises the question of the credibility or validity of the accusation itself. It is perhaps because of this lack of credibility that some critics have suggested that the moral and ethical overtones of the trial are indeed a mask for its underlying political motivation. The accusation is an extremely serious one and some of the attorneys for the prosecution have even made connections with the infamous Nazi laboratories, the Nuremberg trials and the heinous Apartheid regime in South Africa. Such a connection is evident given that African and European patients in Dr Seller's hospital were segregated on the basis of race which is, incidentally, similar to the kind of blatant segregationist and racist practices prevalent in the colonial period. One would expect, therefore, that, in a case with such political and ethical ramifications, the legal proceedings would reflect that seriousness both in the judicious selection process of the witnesses, the 'meticulous preparation' by the defence attorneys, and the content and manner in which the material is presented in court.

However, the text subverts all the expectations by introducing a host of witnesses from diverse backgrounds seemingly randomly selected. The list of witnesses for the prosecution includes, a madman, a religious zealot, a clown, a traditional healer, a war veteran, a narcissist, a deaf and mute, a politician, etc., each telling their own story. In the process of story-telling, each digresses into complex, even if incomplete commentaries on philosophy, metaphysics, politics, different religions, law, society, and histories that have no direct rapport with the central story. Moreover, these incomplete and somewhat irrelevant stories to the central story help to 'desacralise', as it were, the courtroom by turning it into what a judge in *Le Procès du muet* has called a '*théâtre du boulevard*', (popular drama) that is, a stage for the dramatic presentation of farce with all the humour and laughter.

For instance the first witness to testify for the prosecution is Libassi, a war veteran whose broken French and manner of expression would reduce even the most serious, most orderly courtroom into fits of laughter. Here is how he introduces himself even before they swear him in: '*le nom pour moi y'a na Libassi Janvier, mère pour été né moi le janvier et le père pour moi le nom-là. Moi y'a na ancien combattant, moi fait la guerre, moi y'a na quatre galons caporal, moi été voir le général Di Gaulle, moi y'a na avec le photo avec lui*' (p. 105).[10] When asked to raise his right hand to swear in, he raises the left; and when the judge asks jokingly to raise his stronger hand, he retorts, '*la main pour moi qui y'a na forte, voilà lui (en montrant la main gauche) . . .*' And ironically, he tells the court that he was working as an interpreter for Dr Seller: '*métier pour moi y'a na deux; moi chazeur de caïman et moi intépété pour patron*' (p. 106).[11] It is with this statement that the judge dismisses him. By introducing such a character-witness whose testimony creates humour, laughter, irony, both in terms of his broken French and his hilarious gestures, the text attempts to demystify the atmosphere of awe that prevails in and around a courtroom, that is, the kind of aura that is marked by solemnity, strict observance of rules and rituals.

It has been said that misunderstanding is the source of all comedy. That is the case with one of the witnesses named Yangoye Pascal, the clown. His duty in the accused's estate is to take care of the animals and in particular of two of the animals, a deer and a giraffe named Elizabeth and Françoise. But during the cross-examination, the witness simply refers to the animals rather affectionately by their human names. His attribution of human names to the animals without clarification becomes a source of misunderstanding because the judges, the attorneys and the court audience do not have any hint that would contradict their assumption that Elizabeth and Françoise are humans. When the witness tells the court that his wife had suggested they eat Elizabeth, the judge reacts sternly: '*c'est de l'anthropophagie criminelle! Cela vous aurez valu, à tous les deux, des années de prison*' (p. 113).[12]

When the accused intervenes to tell the court of the death of Elizabeth and the illness of Françoise the exchange between him and the judge helps to reveal the source of the misunderstanding. That is, while the witness had been talking about animals in his testimony, the judge and the court audience had been thinking that he was referring to actual people. When the judge asks what the young people died of '*et de quoi sont mortes ces jeunes personnes?*' the accused asks which young people, and the judge replies, '*Françoise et Elizabeth voyons!*' The accused then rather mockingly sets things right, that they are his deer and his giraffe: '*mais Françoise et Elizabeth étaient simplement ma biche et ma girafe.*' (p. 114). This draws a thunder of laughter from the audience and with that another witness is dismissed. In both cases, the witnesses' testimonies do not shed any light on the central story per se since they seem to dilute it by multiplying secondary stories. However, those stories, as we have seen, bring some comic relief to a highly emotional trial.

While those two witnesses digress from the central story in order to create comedy, others tackle issues that, though not directly related to the case in point, do raise serious legal, historical, and religious questions. For example, Imam Samba, a religious zealot digresses to a critical commentary on Judeo-Christian dogmatism and hegemony. He declares, '*les catholiques embrouillaient la compréhension de l'écriture sainte . . . La doctrine, les attributs métaphysiques et positifs de leur Dieu, l'hégémonie cléricale, les coutumes sociales, tout . . .*' (p. 135).[13] As a professed sceptic, he takes to task Cartesian logic by questioning the logicality of the whole episode of the alleged betrayal of Christ and the subsequent chastisement of Judas Iscariot. In his re-enactment of that episode, he acts as a self-appointed defence attorney in Judas's trial.

Samba's first argument is that if Jesus had been destined to die in order to save the world, then there would be no point or rather no logic in presenting the case as if Judas had been responsible for Jesus's death through the alleged betrayal. He questions, '*pourquoi parler de trahison comme si la mort du Christ était imprévisible? On savait que le Christ devait un jour mourir pour sauver le monde*' (p. 143).[14] By questioning the episode and other aspects of the Bible such as the crucifixion and the resurrection of Christ and the icons that characterise the Christian religion, the Imam is questioning the very basis of the Western religious and moral principles and belief systems.

Samba does not understand how Judas could have betrayed Jesus for the meagre sum of thirty 'deniers' given that he was the treasurer of the group. Samba's contention is that if Judas had been in need of money as implied in the accusation against him, he would simply have escaped with all the money: '*si c'était un homme si intéressé, si vénal, comme cela est traditionnellement admis, il aurait emporté le trésor en sa possession, au lieu de se contenter de cette maigre pitance*' (p. 143).[15] Moreover, Samba argues that if Jesus had foreknowledge of his betrayal and had even told one of his disciples about it, then that disciple and all others who knew about it and did nothing to help him, should be charged with failing to assist someone in need; they should be charged with complicity: '*ne pensez-vous pas que dans le procès de Judas, il y aurait lieu de poursuivre Jean et même tous les autres apôtres pour complicité d'assassinat sur la personne de leur maître Jésus?*' He questions, '*quand le Christ a été arrêté, aucun apôtre ne l'a secouru; n'y a t-il pas eu là, ce que vous, homme de loi, appelez la non-assistance à une personne en danger?*' (p. 143)[16]

Samba is sceptical of the fact that someone of the stature and with the powers of Jesus was unknown to his adversaries especially since Judas had to kiss him as a way to identify him to his enemies. His conclusion is that Judas should be seen not so much as a traitor as he has been branded by the scriptures but rather as a victim, indeed a scapegoat. Samba uses the trial of Judas both to question the validity of certain beliefs that have been 'naturalised' as facts and the logicality of the episode of the alleged betrayal of Jesus. Once more this witness's critical re-evaluation of certain philosophical and religious issues has no direct connection with the accusation against Dr Seller, though as a religious figure himself, questioning some of the basis of his beliefs is questioning his own morality. But in such a case in which clear and direct testimonies are imperative, setting in motion such an endless process of reasoning on issues not related to the central story, is again an attempt to divert attention away from the case itself as a way to subvert the legal process. In addition, Samba's criticism of the process of reasoning or as he himself says, of '*logique cartésienne*' (Cartesian logic) that is very pertinent in the Western legal process and the imported legal processes in post-colonial Africa, seems to defer permanently any attempt to arrive at a verdict.

Trials as metaphor

It is perhaps this type of digression into commentaries on philosophy, religion, law, ethics, etc. that has led Posner to suggest, in his reading of law and Western literatures, that legal stories are used in works of fiction as metaphors. As he writes, 'law as depicted in literature is often just a metaphor for something else that is the primary concern of author and reader' (p. 15). In this case, Le Procès du muet may be read as a metaphor for the trial of Africa and its corrupt leadership. As one of the judges has pointed out, 'nous avons à juger . . . un échantillon représentatif des cadres africains dégénérés. Pass Yam était ministre à Djandjan. Biga Zansoiba, inspecteur des douanes, nommé à la tête de l'Union Economique Africaine ne s'est donné pour mission que de créer le cafouillis . . . Il voyage à tout vent, accumule les frais de mission . . . Les pauvres paient pour eux' (pp. 115–16).[17]

Both texts do raise ethical issues. Le Procès du muet uses corruption and embezzlement to raise those issues. Le Procès d'un Prix Nobel raises the moral question of using human beings in medical research even if the findings in such research might be of benefit to humanity as a whole. But because Dr Seller is an international figure and an expatriate from a former European colonial power, some critics of the text have contended that Dr Seller's trial is indeed politically motivated. The preface by Guy Daninos is appropriately titled 'Le Procés d'un Prix Nobel de Séraphin Ndaot: Est-il un procès politique?' (The Trial of a Nobel Laureate by Séraphin Ndaot: Is it a Political Trial?) in which he writes,

> le fait est que le procès intenté au docteur Seller se présente plutôt comme un procès politique: autrement dit, l'ancien colonisé se vengerait sur le docteur Seller de l'ex-colonisateur, dont il condamne l'assistance technique tout en jugeant indispensable, la coopération étant considérée comme une forme de néo-colonialisme; . . . Dès lors la cause profonde de ce procès serait à rechercher dans l'inconscient collectif (p. 5).[18]

In addition to raising ethical and political issues, Dr Seller's conduct does also lend itself to a cultural or indeed racial criticism. Textual evidence clearly shows that there were many patients of European origin at his hospital at the time that he is alleged to have selectively used his African patients as guinea pigs in his experiments. One can even read further into the trial as an attempt to expose the conspiracy of some countries mainly in the West to use Africans as guinea pigs or as scapegoats. One may cite, for instance, the malicious conspiracy to link the origins of AIDS to Africa, the use of the African continent as a dumping ground for nuclear and other forms of wastes generated by the West.

As a religious leader, his trial might also be read as that of the Christian missionaries whose cultural invasion of Africa paved the way for a colonialist adventurism that systematically undermined Africans' rights and decimated their civilisations. But these various issues seem to be undermined by the fact that the trial itself is a systematic subversion of the story-telling-interpretation processes which would have led to a verdict.

The deferral of judgement/justice

One such subversion is the death of the prosecuting lawyer and the accused towards the end of the trial when a verdict would have been appropriate. Both die, ironically, from 'okolo', a disease on which the accused had worked throughout his life and for which he had found a cure. Their deaths at that strategic point validate the argument made earlier that the trial is not teleological. The trial simply sets up a situation in which a resolution is permanently deferred. When the judge declares following the death of the accused that there will be no final statements, no pleading and no verdict '*il n'y aura ni réquisitoire, ni plaidoirie, ni verdict*,' he is indeed confirming what has been obvious throughout the trial, that is, the impossibility of arriving at a verdict.

Even though the trial of the corrupt officials in *Le Procès du muet* ends in the conviction of the accused, the question still remains as to how the presiding judge arrived at the verdict given that the defendants opted for silence. Of course, it could be said that the evidence against the accused was quite clear, except that at no point during the trial did the court show any concrete evidence. Even the testimony of the secretary who worked for both of the accused does not incriminate them to the extent that they can be convicted since she, as other witnesses, tells her own story that does not shed any light on the central story. The silence of the accused does not give the judge the stories that might help her to come to a decision. There are no indications, perhaps because it is a criminal case, that the defendants had told their stories to notaries (as reliable witnesses) who then sent their transcripts to the judge (as is the case in the judicial processes in some African countries). The conviction of the narrator's father at the same time as the other two, or actually the simulacrum of the father even though he was not in court, seems to suggest that the verdict might have come from some other sources than the presiding judge.

If we take into account the fact that in many African societies death is never a natural occurrence but generally believed to be triggered by some invisible forces, then the death of the accused might be interpreted, not so much as a result of medical complications, but as a verdict or punishment by those forces. The constant reference to the ancestors, *'pardonnez, ancêtres, à votre serviteur de n'avoir pas su à temps décoder votre message . . .'* (p. 229)[19] by the narrator's uncle at this point of the trial would suggest those forces are the deities and the ancestors of the society of Galemba who are furious that their posterity has been used as subjects in medical research.

Conclusion

What follows from the discussions above is that any interpretation of legal stories in African works of fiction must take into consideration not only the ethical, social, political and cultural contexts of production of the texts, but more importantly the role of the ancestors. Their spirits are believed to be omnipresent in the society and they might be considered as real judges working, as they do, behind the scenes. In that case, the presiding judges in both trials and all the participants are acting as marionnettes used by the deities to create a semblance of a trial, to set up a legal situation, to subvert the decision-making process and, at the end, render some sort of 'divine justice'. Nevertheless, to make this divine justice appear as if rendered by the judges in the trials, the texts present it in terms similar to what Max Weber has called 'kadijustiz' and cited here by Lawrence Rosen as a 'form of judicial legitimacy in which judges never refer to a settled group of norms or rules but are simply licensed to decide each case according to what they see as its individual merits' (p. 59).

NOTES

The notes that follow are translations of the French citations in the text. In translations 11 and 12 below, I have tried to maintain the pidginisation of French in the English translation and also tried to capture the humour from the French. All the translations are mine.

1. African traditional societies instituted self-examining rules that forced each individual to question his/her conscience.
2. All he has to do to liberate his soul is to speak. Only truth can appease his conscience.
3. I repeat that your court must think in absolute serenity and declare itself incompetent to try this case.
4. It is now your duty to report to the peoples of the Union, those who elected you to act on their behalf . . . You ought to remain a responsible man to the end.
5. You are a very high African official, you are the founding president of Club of Friends of Sahelian countries, you are an economist. You are a former minister of planning and development of Djandjan. Could you give us your own conception of African development?
6. The accused here present are the garbage of our African societies, dangerous beasts that have caused destruction in their divagations . . . Perhaps Pass Yam has invested the stolen money in drugs. As a minister, he was involved in illegal trafficking in diamonds . . . Both accused are the very prototypes of corrupt rotten civil servants . . . M. Biga Zansoiba, you are sick, you are suffering from financial bulimia. You are a delinquent . . . As for you M. Pass Yam, you are a rare bird. Let's say that you are charged with all the sins.
7. There is not one single Truth, but truths; each person has his/her own version of truth. Between psychic and material truths, there is a fundamental and objective truth . . .
8. Is the mission of the attorney not the relentless quest for truth?
9. . . . in an indefinite period of time, administered to his patients substances not recommended by medical sciences. He is also accused of having used his patients in experiments in the process of which all of the patients died.
10. Name for me is Libassi Janvier, mother gave me birth on January and father gave me that name. I am a war veteran. I made the war, I have four decorations, I been see general Di Gaulle, I in picture with him.
11. The hand for me that is strong that's him (showing his left hand) . . . job for me is two; me hunter of cayman and me interpreter for boss.

12. That's criminal anthropophagy! That would have earned both of you some years in jail.
13. Catholics made the Holy Scriptures obscure ... The doctrine, the metaphysical and positive attributes of their God, clerical hegemony, social norms, all ...
14. Why talk of betrayal as if Jesus's death had not been predicted? It was a well known fact that Christ would one day die to save the world.
15. Had he been such an interested and venal man as traditionally believed, he would have escaped with all the money in his possession rather than stealing the meagre sum that he is accused of.
16. Don't you think that in Judas's trial, there are grounds to charge John and all other disciples of complicity in the murder of their master Jesus? ... when Christ was arrested, none of his apostles came to his rescue, wasn't that a case of what you, men of law, call failing to assist someone in need?
17. We have on trial ... a representative sample of degenerated African officials. Pass Yam was minister in Djandjan. Biga Zansoiba, Custom's Inspector, appointed to head the African Economic Union, had as his mission to create chaos ... He travels all over, accumulates out of station allowances ... The destitute pay for them.
18. The fact is that the trial of Dr Seller is seen more as a political trial: in which case the former colonised is retaliating on Dr Seller, from the former colonial power, whose technical assistance is condemned even though it is indispensable, cooperation being considered as a form of neo-colonialism ... Then the deeper cause of the trial must be rooted in the collective unconscious.
19. Ancestors, forgive your servant for having failed to decode your warning message in time ...

WORKS CITED

Aluko, T. M. Wrong Ones in the Dock. (London: Heinemann, 1982).

Bennett, Lance. 'Storytelling in Criminal Trials: A Model of Social Judgement', The Quarterly Journal of Speech, 64 (1978).

Conley, M. John and William M. O'Barr. Rules Versus Relationships: the Ethnography of Legal Discourse. Chicago: University of Chicago Press, 1989.

Derrida, Jacques. Interview in Criticism in Society, 164, Imre Saluzinszky, ed. (New York: Methuen, 1987), cited by Sanford Levinson and Steven Mailloux, eds, in Interpreting Law and Literature: A Hermeneutic Reader (Evanston, Illinois: Northwestern University Press, 1988).

Goodrich, Peter. Legal Discourse: Studies in Linguistics. Rhetoric and Legal Analysis. (New York: MacMillan Press, 1987).

Ilboudo, Patrick. Le Procès du muet (Ouagadougou: Editions la Mante, 1987). All references are from this edition and page numbers are in parentheses in the text.

Levinson, Sanford and Steven Mailloux. Interpreting Law and Literature: A Hermeneutic Reader. (Evanston, Illinois: Northwestern University Press, 1989).

Leyh, Gregory. 'Dworkin's Hermeneutics', *Mercer Law Review*, 39, 3 (Spring 1988).

Ndaot, Séraphin. *Le Procès d'un Prix Nobel* (Paris: La Pensée Universelle, 1983). All references are from this edition and page numbers are in parentheses in the text.

Nkashama, Pius. *Ecritures et discours littéraires: étude sur le roman africain.* (Paris: L'Harmattan, 1989).

Posner, Richard. *Law and Literature: A Misunderstood Relation.* (Cambridge, Mass.: Harvard University Press, 1988).

Rosen, Lawrence. *The Anthropology of Justice: Law as Culture in Islamic Society.* (Cambridge: Cambridge University Press, 1989).

Towards Feminist Aesthetics in Nigerian Drama: The Plays of Tess Onwueme

Olu Obafemi

The critical enterprise is, at least, a response to and a consequence of creative productivity, and at best, a catalyst and galvaniser of creativity. Creativity itself, in spite of large-scale pretensions otherwise among formalists and structuralists,[1] is determined and conditioned by sociological factors; social reality. Within the framework of this assertion therefore, any form of criticism; classic, bourgeois, Marxist and feminist, can of necessity only be a reflection, a refraction and a propelling interpretation of the creative production that has emerged from the material reality of the cosmos in which it is produced.

Talking of feminist criticism in Africa (specifically in Nigeria) and with particular reference to literary and dramatic productions, it is not an accident that feminist critical thought has not gone beyond preliminary stages of discourse. This is essentially because, most creative output, especially within the ambience of the theatrical medium, has hardly focused on feminist concerns. This statement must however not be construed to imply that feminism is alien to the contemporary African society, and hence not a fertile terrain to pre-occupy dramatic cultural workers. The point being made here is that as a result of the prevalent nature of the systematic obfuscation of ideological perceptions of society – a deliberate mystification by the political system in aid of the perpetration of the status quo – clear ideological positions and trends are yet to gain objective appreciation, tolerance of expression, and responsiveness from the dominant socio-political system.[2] Without intending to belabour this observation, since it is on its own an issue requiring serious and thorough scholarly attention, we clarify here that

issues relating to ideology have attracted the greatest pejora-
tion in political brackets in the so-called Third World, such
that in Nigeria for example, to seek political and intellectual discourse along ideological parameters – be it bourgeois,
Marxist or feminist – is to generate suspicion and invite imputed
motives.

Our intention, therefore, to undertake political discourse of
Tess Onwueme's search for an appropriate dramaturgy and
aesthetics for her creative perception of contemporary society,
local and global, along feminist lines is to indicate the vitality of
the feminist critical enterprise, or any other ideological enterprise
for that matter in assessing the writer's relevance to the sociological reality of his or her environment. We must quickly add
here that neither is Tess Onwueme a self-proclaimed feminist, nor
is the critic under any mandate to clarify the writer's ideological
penchant before interpreting the artist's work to the advantage of
art and society. In this regard, Wole Soyinka recently reminded
critics of the independent nature of the critical discipline when
he said that 'critical writing constitutes an independent source of
satisfaction' from creativity.[3]

I would like to take off with a factual statement that feminism
as an active ideological preoccupation does not really exist
concretely in Nigeria, the way it does in Europe and America.
Apart from 'Women in Nigeria', a fledgling feminist organisation
yet to implant its relevance on the social consciousness of the
Nigerian people, the only remarkable women's organisation to
whom most of the initiative of popular mobilisation belongs is
the largely reactionary body called the National Council of
Nigerian Women.[4] By this token, feminist criticism has yet to
evolve into a critical discipline in Nigeria. It is no wonder that
in almost all the journals and sustained studies on feminist
thinking and writing, there is hardly any mention of Africa. Such
is the paucity of information on the feminist experience of the
black people that I was intrigued as well as amused reading a
major study recently, on feminism. The book has only one chapter on Black Feminism – and that chapter was shared with
Lesbianism. With copious apology.[5] The only other parenthetical factual statement that I should make here is that, to date,
there are only two notable female dramatists in Nigeria whose
works have received considerable critical attention.[6] It is

important just to mention the obvious: concern with women in Nigerian literature is not the domain of the female sex alone. Indeed, the most radical treatment of women's intervention in the socio-economic history of Nigeria is by male dramatists;[7] and this has nothing really to do with the masculinist nature of the society since these creative interventions are tellingly dialectical.[8]

Our concern with the perception of feminist criticism will be on the level of the representation of women's experience in literature regarding the treatment of the objective conditions of women; their socio-cultural products as well as their material being as related to the complexities of the macro experience in society. An extention of this perception is our examination of how feminist concerns are transposed into literature, without triteness, contrivance and without compromising aesthetic quality as a way of giving validation to the literary and theatrical value of the concerns. In other words, we shall focus on the way in which feminist concerns are treated or ought to be treated with demonstrable concern for both the cultural production as well as the text as literary product; a concern with sociology as well as the textual surface of literature (aesthetic quality including symbols, metaphor, language and structure). The essence is to distinguish between epistemological polemic which is located in mode of production alone and the aesthetic stratagems of production. Indeed, Michelle Barrett, another feminist of note has asserted that feminist literary criticism should be concerned with the identification of 'levels of aesthetic skill in the construction of works of art'.[9] This project cannot be more germane for the critical standards employed to interpret the 'novel' ideological praxis of feminism in Nigeria and the maturing output of Tess Onwueme.

In examining the works of Onwueme, from the standpoint of the dialectic interplay of conscious creation and the critic's interpretation of it, the early part of her still young dramatic output are consciously feminist. They reveal a dramatist's pre-occupation with the travails and setbacks of women in a traditionally patriarchal society. We will show briefly in this essay that, at this stage of her creative inquiry her work is amateurish, racy and tentative, both in content and technique, but simmering with potential and imaginative bubble. I have actually stated elsewhere that her first two published plays *A Hen Too Soon* and *The Broken Calabash*,[10] both of which deal with the feminist question – the heroine in each of the plays revolts violently against the restrictions placed on her liberties by a masculinist tradition – lack visionary focus and technical deftness.[11] First, a brief summary of the plots of *A Hen Too Soon* and *The Broken Calabash* before concentrating on the plays which form the task of this essay; *The Desert Encroaches* and *Ban Empty Barn*.[12]

A Hen Too Soon is a play about defiance of imbedded patriarchy and the consequence of such assertiveness. It is also about the heroine's attempt to break away from fossilising tradition in order to achieve freedom of will and action. An eighteen-year-old girl, Gladys is compelled to marry Oboli, a man twice her age, who turns out to be impotent. Unable to cope with the situation, Gladys turns to Oboli's son who impregnates her, thus breaking the taboo. Their breach of taboo and custom drives them to elope rather than face the communal rite of expiation by punishment.

The protagonist of her second play, *The Broken Calabash*, shows a bit more forcefulness, strength of character and will. Ona, is an undergraduate and an only child. By tradition, as an only issue, she must marry within the community and propagate it. Alternatively, she could marry another lady into the family and thus gain her own freedom. This is also a repelling option for her. Her final option of getting married to an outsider also collapses as a result of the overbearing interference and encroachment by her father, Courtuma. Her lover, Diaku is frustrated as their affair has degenerated into a hide-and-seek romance. In his despair, he marries Ona's best friend. Ona holds her father responsible for the destruction of her dreams and in a bid for revenge, sleeps with an unknown and socially inconsequential person, and becomes pregnant. This act is unbearable for her tradition-bound father who commits suicide.

In these two plays, one finds Onwueme's thrust as one of commitment to the course of a radical transformation of static tradition and hidebound customs in the contemporary age. She pursues this concern through the advocation of the female component of humanity in her society. As we have noted earlier her feminist anxieties are compromised by artistic raciness, plottal contrivance and structural unevenness, all of which weaken the delivery of her message. It is significant that within the feminist frame

of reference, the level of vision reached in these plays only rein-
forces, albeit inadvertently, the dominant hierarchichal ethos
whereas, what is required is not mere negation but a 'reconstructive movement' which transcends the expression of dissatisfaction
with the status quo.[13] In spite of this, it is impossible not to be
held by the incipient talent and creative potential that one is compelled to notice in these early works.

To Dialectical Inquiry

Onwueme's two serious plays, on which this study significantly
rests, demonstrate very strong evidence of self discovery, both
on the level of dramaturgy as well as on the level of creative
vision. She departs remarkably from facile feminism and linear
plotting to grapple with larger and more engaging themes of
national and international importance, revealing an indomitable
scope of female contribution to the task of shaping a materialist
consciousness of the immediate and extended universes, beyond
the familiar course of a certain kind of amorphous holism and
idyllism in African humanities.[14] Her real contribution as a
female dramatist begins to emerge in these two plays, *The Desert
Encroaches* and *Ban Empty Barn* where she employs allegory as
a metaphoric and satiric idiom to handle highly political and committed themes.

On the level of statement, the plays fall within the frame of
reconstructive materialism.[15] Both plays explore the dominance
of a capitalist social order erected upon the systematic exploitation of the productive sector of society (the proletariat and the
peasantry). The plays' fictive world represents a predatory structure which materially and psychologically alienates the working
majority. It also materially impoverishes them. Increased productivity almost directly equates with increased poverty. The bourgeoisie, which determine and control the production strategy as
well as the distribution mechanism utilise their hegemonic status
to maximise profit for themselves to the detriment of the labour
force. What emerges as the play advances, from this social contradiction, inexorably, is distinct patterns of class relations, class
consciousness and polarisation among the social groups; the elite
minority and the proletarian-peasant majority. The dialectic of

such a situation is the emergence of oppositional relationships along clear lines of struggle for the attainment of self-liberation and radical transformation of society by the underprivileged majority, on the one hand, and the sustenance of dominance by the establishment.

The *Desert Encroaches* examines the nature of the operation of international monopoly capitalism from the standpoint of dialectical materialism, while *Ban Empty Barn* focuses on the state of the neo-colonial dependent capitalist socio-economic order in the contemporary Nigerian society. In both plays, Onwueme identifies the inevitability of violence and struggle in such an exploitative and inegalitarian order as capitalism. The Leninist dictum of the apparatus of dislodgement being inherent in the character of the capitalist order is dramatised in these plays. Oppression generates rejection and ultimate rebellion in human nature. We also find starkly manifest the inherence of the logic and mechanism of exploitation in international politics where the industrialised nations manipulate the underdeveloped ones for continuing exploitation.

In *The Desert Encroaches*, the weak labouring animals of the South (south here geo-politically refers to the Southern hemisphere, although there is an ethnically narrow sense in which it can refer to Southern Nigeria)[16] are the true generators and producers of the material economy of the fictive animal kingdom. Yet, they are forced to eke out a mean pittance for bare existence at the end of laborious industry. Another acute situation deplored in the play is the net appropriation of the arable farmlands by Northern animals (reference to the industrialised, powerful nations in the Northern hemisphere) to cater for the agricultural and manufacturing requisites of their own kingdom. Denied the benefit of the returns from their productivity, their natural resources appropriated, the Southern animals live in a sorry state of abjection, famine and deprivation. Lumpenism, vagrancy and beggarism characterise the social atmosphere in their kingdom. It is perhaps unnecessary to embark here on the simple translation of the picture painted here into a one-to-one equivalent of the economic reality in a capitalist economy. The reality in the Third World makes such an exercise unnecessary. The dynamic of its dramatic representation in this play suffices. Donkey, a Southern animal which recalls the role and image of Benjamin the donkey in

Orwell's *Animal Farm* aptly captures the contradiction of social relations in a capitalist economy;

> ... the flood of my sweat and blood
> On the fields tilling and ploughing. The earth
> I mine, the seeds I man
> But at harvest I am manned
> To trade my lot and load for their luxury (*Desert*, p. 31)

The dialectic of the situation is further captured in a dialogue between the leadership of the Southern animals about their state of existence during which the sheer echo of the Lion's voice representing the Northern animals impresses the dominance of their oppressive status. The Southern animals are here represented by Donkey, Tortoise and Dog:

> Donkey: Why must they make our labour so hard, so
> hard in vain. Drawing water from wells.
> Whilst they barn in millions, billions and
> trillions of the fluids and resources of that
> atomic cauldron?
>
> Lion's huge voice on stage:
> It is the symbol of our power
> The mark of our greatness, power and glory ... (*Desert*)

The antagonism, the Hegelian dialectic of thesis and antithesis in the oppressor–oppressed relation sets the stage for the materialist dialectic vision which proposes the inevitable essence of resolution through confrontation and collective struggle. This is mimetically enacted via the sword combat between the leadership of the Northern animals symbolised by Lion with members of his class lined up behind him (Wolf, Hyena, etc.) and the representatives of the oppressed Southern animals backed by Fox, Tortoise, Dog etc. The strength of this episode is that it is not a simplistic exhibition of opposites; not a Manichean divide, as some animals from the Southern camp remain 'non-aligned' in the combat. They include such perpetually milked animals as the Cow (iconising wilful exploitation) and some others like Dove (naturally a peaceful animal) seek arbitration. Indeed, Dove supplies universal preachment of liberal non-meaning oneness and a need for armistice:

> Dove: Animals of the four winds
> Quench the flames in your hearts

> Surrender the fangs of your pride . . .
> Unite . . . let the left hand wash the right
> hand,
> and the right hand, the left hand giving the
> world a heart to feel
> with its heart and stand on its feet today (*Desert*, p. 41).

This is a plea for moderation, the familiar 'non-violence' approach to concrete issues; an amorphous solidarity and ineffable spiritual oneness in a world split down the middle by materialist antagonism.

The rest of the play is a dramatic discourse of the nature of neo-colonialism in which the developed countries of the North perpetrate economic domination over the Third World (animals of the South). The play stresses the criminal collusion of some Southern animals – the new national bourgeoisie occupying the cushioned hierarchy of the social stratum. Tortoise inveighs against that middle-class elite who turn themselves into subservient 'dogs', tyrannising over their own citizens in order to maintain a convenient and totally docile relationship with the superpowers:

> Tortoise: Our dogs are servile
> They bark and bark at the moons at us
> and threaten the wind their brethren with
> their growl. But to the masters they wag
> their
> tail as the masters eat (*Desert*, p. 33)

Political intimidation and repression evolves to silence criticism, dissent and signs of struggle against the social ethos. Decrees, arbitrary detention of labour leaders, students and progressive individuals form the operational strategy of state superstructures, mainly to enhance domination and hegemonic perpetuation of the status quo. Political and economic alienation of the deprived majority is the common logistics of operation by the political elite. This exacerbates the polarity in social relations as the majority grow in poverty whilst the elite roll in dismal opulence. The point of psycho-social alienation is well made:

> The farmer and his wife are always quarrelling
> over food
> and milk and yam. They fight . . .
> whilst the rich live in excessive hedonism.

what do you associate with rich people?
Enjoyment
My drinking, dancing, winning ... (Desert)

This state of inequality makes a revolutionary confrontation inevitable. But this struggle, the play counsels, has to be based on seminal indoctrination and conscientisation of the oppressed animal class – the militant youth. This pedagogic process was championed by Tortoise (who in tradition symbolises tricksterism, wisdom and cunning). This awareness vanguard yields dividends as the animals resolve to 'fight to reclaim their stolen wealth'. The forceful and militant youth compel the predator-class from the North to accept the reality of the struggle. The animal chorus, is led symbolically by Dog, usually servile and faithful:

Chorus: Yes, we have come to force our leaders
         to accept peace.

Tortoise: Yes, dogs have risen to say they no
         longer will eat bones. Dogs too
         Like flesh. And the tortoise no
         Longer crawls, it now jumps and leaps (Desert, p. 75)

Resolution must be compelled, not negotiated, through revolutionary action.

The theme of revolutionary struggle and resistance to exploitation and oppression is continued in her next play, Ban Empty Barn. Here again, the allegorical strategy is the dominant dramatic device. Bene and Bede, the main 'duo-personae' of the play are chicks set on challenging the perpetration of poverty and deprivation in the fictive world of the play called Hungaria (Hunger area?). They question the quality of life in their segment of the fabular world and demand democracy from the political elite. The focus in the play is not on international issues, but the socio-economic order in the playwright's immediate geo-polity, Nigeria. The protagonist duo, together with their mother are frustrated in their futile search for food. Economic down-turn via recession has left the barn in a state of depletion. Middlemen, agents of exploitation have swindled the man who is their breadwinner and he is unable to provide for the family. Family squabbles and rifts become incessant. Their immediate neighbour the priest, wallows in opulence and comfort. He lives so lavishly that his domestic animals are fattened and can choose what to eat. The chicks question this wide disparity in their relative state of existence. The scale of oppression in this fictive world follows a hierarchy. The priest symbolising the predatory elite oppresses the mothers who in turn oppress their own children.

Dramatic Technique: Allegory as Dialectic Inquiry

I have advanced earlier that in Onwueme's plays which venture and project beyond facile feminism to engage in a materialist perception of society – national and universal – we experience an unrelenting search for aesthetic and technical resource which reveal an ambitious experimentation with form. Indeed, Onwueme does not hesitate to acknowledge the influence and inspiration she received from experimental playwrights of the middle generation of the dramatic scenario in Nigeria such as Femi Osofisan.[17] This inspiration is not just in the area of social vision and political commitment, but in terms of the interminable search for the appropriate popular dramaturgic idiom and form to express her social vision. Osofisan is himself most anxious to express the need for artists of the materialist bent to continue to seek a balance between the aesthetic constituents of art (a sensorial way of articulating and transmitting) and radical politics which preoccupy their creative enterprise.[18] From *The Desert Encroaches*, Onwueme's first play to catch popular literary attention having won the annual prize for drama in the 1985 Association of Nigerian Authors (ANA) award, the playwright has continued to probe, frenziedly, for politically sensitive themes shaped with remarkable craft.

In this vein, we find her employment of the allegorical mechanism as a symbolic and metaphoric route to social satirisation and dialectical inquiry of contemporary society, of tremendous impact on the contribution of female dramatists in Nigeria. This form – the fabular and the allegorical – are newly and refreshingly re-deployed on the Nigerian dramatic scene. They have, of course, been used earlier by theatre practitioners in Nigeria, especially by Kola Ogunmola and Hubert Ogunde; proponents of vernacular (popular) theatre in Nigeria. Onwueme's recourse to the device is innovative in the literary sub-field of Nigerian theatre.

Allegory would conventionally refer in literature to an extended metaphor wherein characters, objects, icons, incidents and descriptions assume polysemic proportions; carrying 'one or more sets of fully developed meanings in addition to the apparent literary ones'.[19] In these plays, allegory has been employed in the post Lafontaine and Orwellian traditions through animal fables to make pungent satiric comments on national and global politics. The device is used to make a satirical reference to a materialist view and exploration of an exploitative and oppressive social order in the throes of seminal liberatory struggle. On the local level, her discourse is centred on the dominance of a monetarist economy which provides a bi-polar social relation and consciousness, indicating the inexorability of revolutionary action. On the international scene, which itself is a macro extension of the national, the playwright employs allegory as a satiric tool to restate the imminence of global extinction posed by nuclear armament and technological sophistication dangled over the lethal face of the world by power blocs.

There are three noteworthy areas of dramatic technique where the satirical implications of her use of allegory help our perception of her vision; characterisation, setting and action. Climatically and vegetationally, the South inhabits the rain forest belt of plentiful rainfall and thick mangrove forest. Its dryness is a pointed irony aimed at the forces of exploitation and plunder visited upon it by the North – the Western Euro-American powers who encroach on it ensuring its desertification. As the plays allegorise, the advanced industrial world supervises the 'environmental depletion' of the South. The encroaching desert is the multifaceted exploitation by Euro-American capitalism via the agency of neo-colonialism.

On the level of setting, the play is situated in the thick forest, with shrub undergrowths (Desert, p. 18). Note that the undergrowth states the nature of the under-development of the South. Dialectically, the huge Southern forest obstructs photosynthesis (the energy-deriving source) for the shrubs. This leads to stunted growth and eventual atrophy. Cosmopolitan countries of the North like America and Britain are the huge trees. The huge Iroko (a giant economy tree at that) waxes strong whilst the shrubs wither.

This is an allegorical statement about the extravagant luxury of the developed countries as the developing countries wallow in impoverishment. The products of the South such as the timbers of the Iroko tree fuel the industrial growth of the North. Still on setting, the play makes a point of the futility of the meeting places and gatherings of world assemblies like the United Nations (UN) controlled by the North. Their pledges in favour of the environment are (meant to be) ineffectual.

The characters in the play embody the antagonistic pattern of relationships. There is high fidelity to the known physiological and 'psychological' constitutions of the animals in their dramatic recreation in the play. Lion is a ferocious, predatory, carnivore. Combined with Hyena an equally strength-studded animal, the image of Northern domination is complete. If Lion stood for America, and Hyena stood for Britain, then the Bear standing for the (now dismantled) USSR introduces a dimension of ideological confusion in the play, because on the one hand, the playwright finds the bear fighting for the weak animals, on the other, it is found to be an imperious, predatory force! The weak animals represent the state of the 'Third World'. They are the source of world resources as well as being the productive forces. The Cow is a milked animal. It does not get to drink from the milk it produces. As in Orwell's *Animal Farm*, the milk ensures the mental health of the elite animals. Mr Dog is the archetype of loyalty, and the hunting machine. He kills the game but is lucky if he gets the bones:

Have I not always been in chains? ...
And my masters, masters of the world,
With these teeth, I serve them
With these paws, I run their errands, and
Execute with my teeth (*Desert*, p. 31)

Mr Dove is the apostle of non-violence; icon of peace. He is naturally averse to confrontation.

But essentially, it is through action, represented in stage direction, that the allegorical message of the play is conveyed. For instance, Movement five's stage direction shows animals in a gathering in which the Southern (lesser) animals are entertaining the carousing and revelling forest leaders with a dance. The centrality of this scene to the whole dramatic situation and the thematic concerns of the play must be fore-grounded. Lion and Bear contest leadership, symbolised by winning the right to sit on the chair, constructed on the backs of the lesser animals – who wince from the weight of the burden they carry (*Desert*, p. 10). The dramatic action in this episode (a) captures the pattern of social relations between the animals, outlining in social reality the way in which economic relations determine social consciousness (b) reveals the mutual suspicion that exists between power-mongering blocs of the world; the intensifying ideological struggle between the Lion, 'capitalist' West and the Bear, 'socialist' East within the Northern hemisphere (again underlining the weakness of the dialectical focus of the play as we mentioned earlier) and (c) highlighting the theme of neo-colonialism in the play.

The thematic weakness mentioned above and elements of technical untidiness, even looseness make the play creak in places. One such element of over-narration is seen in the two legendary birds – Nza and Obu – competing for supremacy. The narration comes at a tempo-spatially inappropriate moment in the play when the central action is being focused on the source of world destruction exemplified by Hiroshima as the dominant instance of dramatic conflict. It is at this point that the birds narrate their hunger strike which virtually led to one emaciating, the other rotting. But this is almost trivial when compared to the playwright's frequent recourse to verbal puns and morphological tricks in moments of dramatic climax. At the moment when the animals are discussing starvation and hunger which also threaten their continued existence, the playwright lapses into a needless and effete play on words

Tortoise:	We must fight
Dog:	For our rice
Tortoise:	Rights. And lies
Dog:	Light?
Ant:	Night
Chorus:	Night. Night. Night.

This amounts to an unnecessary technical and ideological distraction. Fortunately, there is a major improvement on these flaws, if not on thematic rendering in the succeeding play, *Ban Empty Barn*. The play is structurally tight, the allegory more pungent and the sharp satiric effect of the duologue has the potential of stimulating the audience mentally and physically.The pace of the play is fast. Action is sacrificed for dialogue and the characters are highly symbolic. The chick's parents represent the industrious labouring segment of society who cannot even eke out an existence for their dependants. Frustration and despondency result from a declined economy. This is aptly captured in the humorous and satirical dialogue between the agitative chicks, Bede and Nene:

> Bede: Yes, the farmer complains
> Nene: No rain-no grain
> Both: Corn is gone
> Maize is gone
> Wheat is gone
> Rain is gone
> Grain is gone (*Barn*, p. 15)

Hence, the barn is empty; starvation is imminent; all tersely but effectively imaged. Beyond a surface interpretation of this telling satire is the contemporary relevance of the subject matter to the immediate objective reality in the playwright's cosmos. At the time the play was produced, the Nigerian government had just banned the importation of grains, such as rice and wheat, and rice suddenly fell into the category of essential, that is, scarce, commodity. Agriculture had been replaced by oil production and exportation as the monocultural product and source of revenue. Farmers had abandoned their farms to participate in the booming oil industry. The barns were empty and the consequent importation of food depleted foreign reserves.

Another aspect of social reality that comes under sharp criticism is the pattern of power manipulation and power struggle which has come to characterise the political system in Nigeria. It is a system where the essence is not the actual utilisation of power for social upliftment of the lives of the governed, but a preponderance of coups and political changes based on ephemeral values and the libido of the military elite, as in the Nene–Bede/Dede–Keke power tussle and power-mongering in the play. At one point, Dede owns the crown and relishes the power it confers: 'I am King, by virtue of my crown' (p. 56). But he loses both crown and power when Nene knocks him over into the stream and dispossesses him. It is a satiric comment on the political incoherence and social instability generated by constant coups and counter-coups which are not embarked upon out of an altruistic desire to reform society.

What emerges from this examination of Onwueme's plays is a credible feminist view of a contemporary situation beyond a mere concern with sexuality. Here is a fresh female voice addressing the need for a materialist-feminist perspective which demonstrates the productive process of literature as a way of dealing with political issues through an aesthetic use of dramatic technique.

NOTES & REFERENCES

1. Structuralists generally tend to consider sociology in purely marginal and parenthetical terms in relationship to signification which 'is nothing more than the continuously unaccomplished system of systems that reflects back to itself'. Indeed, a leading semiotician, Umberton Eco believes that though subject matter is significant, it is only definable within the theoretical framework of semiotics. See Umberton Eco, *A Theory of Semiotics* (Bloomington: Indiana University Press, 1976).

2. In robust defence of a mystifying liberalism and ideological universalism, which is in itself a political camouflage for the real growth of pseudo-capitalism, the African political elite cast aspersion on clear alternative, especially radical materialist interpretations of society. Pejorative labels are imposed on radical thoughts – labels such as 'extremist', 'subversive' etc. Indeed, recently, the Nigerian Government instructed its Constituent Assembly ratifying the Draft Constitution for a new republic not to include any radical ideological framework as one of the options for a new social order.

3. Indeed, within literary circles in Nigeria, Tess Onwueme's dramatic enterprise as a female playwright, whilst revealing inventiveness and dynamism, has been found 'lean' on feminism. A colleague, Kemi Ilori, a researcher in Nigerian drama who read the original draft of this study, strongly feels that Onwueme 'appears to have more or less settled for those fixed social and "dialogical" parameters – partly trans-gender, partly phallocentric, partly class-orientated – through which a dominantly male society often maintains itself'. My approach is one which makes no pretences to both the extraverted and silent ideological persuasion of the dramatist. I have taken the liberty of a critic to occasionally evaluate a work independently of the views and positions which the artist may or may not hold. This independence of the critic to function creatively and autonomously has been re-affirmed by Wole Soyinka in a keynote address to the 1989 *Calabor Annual International African Literature Conference*, 'Beyond Insularity: Beyond Rushdie: Prescriptions for the Terminal Critica'.

4. This organisation is run and financed largely by well-established, well-connected female members of the middle-class elite in Nigeria with considerable influence on the dominant ruling system. In the absence, or in the ineffectual presence, of a radical feminist movement, this council of women holds sway on women's involvement in national life in Nigeria.

5. Maggie Humn, *Feminist Criticism* (Brighton, Sussex: Harvester, 1986). Note the author's apology and explanation for such disquieting merger of Black Feminism and lesbianism; she says this is premised on the historical fact that most contemporary feminist criticism does not even begin to analyse adequately the experience of Black or lesbian writing.

6. Tess Onwueme is chronologically the second important female playwright in Nigeria, the leading female dramatist being Zulu Sofola, a well-known pioneering Nigerian female playwright whose concerns, visions and dramatic confrontations form an inextricable part of the dominant patriarchal culture and its self-expressive superstructural vocabulary. We have treated her tradition-bound dramatic vision in *Perspectives on Nigerian Literature*, ed. Yemi Ogunbiyi (Lagos: Guardian Books, 1988).

7. Refer, specifically, to the treatment of women in Femi Osofisan's plays. For instance in *Morountodun* (1980) a play which reconstructs the role of the legendary personage, Moremi, who messianically sacrificed herself to save the ruling house of Ile-Ife from the incessant menace of the Igbo invaders. Osofisan recreates the legend in the character of Titubi who commits class suicide in order to enlist her service on the side of the peasant guerrillas in the 1969 Agbekoya revolt in Western Nigeria. Refer also to the present author's *The New Dawn* (Benin: Adena Publishers, 1986) in which the revolutionary radical movement against military dictatorship makes no distinction between genders.

8. These creations evaluate the role of women in purely revolutionary situations when they show dynamism and positiveness in struggle, uninhibited by phallic status.

9. Michelle Barrett, 'Feminism and the Definitive of Cultural Politics' in *Feminism, Culture and Politics* (London: 1982).

10. See my essay on Onwueme in Ogunbiye (ed.) *Perspectives on Nigerian Literature*, 309–13.

11. Tess Onwueme, *A Hen Too Soon* (Owerri: Heins, 1983). *The Broken Calabash* (Owerri: Totan, 1984).

12. Tess Onwueme, *The Desert Encroaches* (Owerri: Heins, 1985). *Ban Empty Barn* (Owerri: Totan, 1986). I have found very reliable and useful Olabisi Koleoso's undergraduate essay on satiric devices in Onwueme's plays (unpublished), Ilorin University, 1989.

13. Janette Reinhert, 'Feminist Theory and Performance' in *Modern Drama*, 32, 1 (March 1989).

14. Such approaches which sacrifice vigorous class analysis and theory for liberal and elusive universalism have been flayed by materialist scholars like Chidi Amuta in his recent book on *The Theory of African Literature* (London: Hans Zell, 1989).

15. 'Reconstructive materialism' captures the position which Michelle Barrett describes as situating positive Marxist-feminism.
16. In effluent socio-political vocabulary in Nigeria, the stereotypic North–South dichotomy is usually manipulated by the ruling class to further perpetrate their hegemony and distract attention from the real economic issues that plague contemporary society.
17. In this fluid periodisation, the creative output of Achebe, Soyinka, Clark, Okigbo, Okara and Ekwensi among others could be taken as the first generation. The succeeding works of Osofisan, Okpewko, Omotoso, Iyayi, Osundare etc. form the high points of the middle generation. New writing of the eighties by writers in their late twenties and early thirties commence the young and third generation of writers, such as Onwueme, Garuba and Irobi.
18. I have quoted in my essay in *African Literature Today*, 12 (1982) that Osofisan's astounding creativity partly results from his quest for a level of writing in which aesthetic profundity embodies correct radical politics.
19. William Rose Benét, *The Readers' Encyclopedia* 3rd ed. (London: A. & C. Black, 1987) 25.

Feminist Inclinations of Flora Nwapa

Ify G. Achufusi

There has been a tendency for African intellectuals to dissociate themselves from the term 'feminism', regarding it as one of those borrowed 'isms' which militate against the development of Africa, perhaps the newest form of neo-colonialism. It is often regarded as some kind of intellectual monstrosity which is geared towards the destruction of the marriage institution in Africa, by straining the 'cordial relationship' between man and woman.

This paper argues that such an attitude arises from a lack of proper understanding of what the term involves. A great deal of the present perception of feminism by women is also a reflection of the deep-seated fear of being rejected by the mainstream, by the privileged section of the society – an effect that has been successfully created and perpetuated through long-lasting socio-cultural intimidation. What has most strongly impacted on this affair, and has negatively affected the development of feminism in Africa generally, is the fact that African societies have not internalised the notion that the woman's self actualisation is no longer dependent on her biological role of reproduction. African societies have reached a point in their history when the most basic tenets and concepts governing the functions and the actual essence of man/woman relationships should be re-examined, so that the position of the woman within the realm of things can be re-evaluated.

Editor's note. Flora Nwapa (born 1931) Nigeria's pioneering woman novelist died in October 1993. She wrote not only adult novels highlighting the plight of women and children but also books especially for children. She founded her own printing press and publishing company – Tana Press and Flora Nwapa Company.

Such a re-evaluation is crucial, especially considering the fact that our society is fast changing and that most of the basic assumptions which direct the said relationships have taken on entirely new shapes and therefore new values. Unfortunately most discourses, social and economic, overlook the very glaring changes in the society and base their analysis of the man/woman relationship on the pre-change situation. Thus, such analysis takes as the norm the very conditions which need to be changed; those oppressive conditions which must disappear in order that the subjugation of more than half the population, the women, may cease.

One such condition is that which bases the woman's value in her society only on her reproductive capability – both the reproduction of actual human beings and that of the labour force,[1] thus recognising this biological function as the woman's only contribution towards the development of her country. Such subsumation limits her self-actualisation and stifles her talents.

In many African states, the above concept has assumed the status of a myth while, the woman herself, in order to maintain eligibility for marriage, or to avoid being isolated and regarded as woman/man, often either restrains herself from discussing the man/woman relationship. When and if she does, rather than analyse the situation from an individual perspective, giving her feeling and reaction to all the limitations imposed on her, she toes exactly those lines prescribed for her by the society. This certainly as Molara Ogundipe-Leslie posits is due to 'the successful intimidation of the African woman by the man'.

She states that:

> Women are shackled by their own negative self-image by centuries of the interiorization of the ideologies of patriarchy. Her own reactions to objective problems therefore are often self-defeating and self-crippling. She reacts with fear, dependency complexes and attitudes to please and cajole where more self-assertive actions are needed.[2]

The African woman urgently needs to rid herself of all the complexes cited above, for although today she is still very much involved in raising the family, she is equally actively participating in other spheres of nation building. To gain recognition in the society therefore, marriage, procreation or selflessly and sheepishly pleasing the man should be neither a pre-requisite nor an imperative. It is therefore very disappointing to note that some of our women feel uncomfortable to declare that they are feminists or to give the impression that they have any connections with feminists or feminist ideology.

Assuming however, that the African woman sees marriage and housewifery as her only source of wish fulfilment, should she shy away from discussing her role as a wife and mother and the pleasures and tribulations involved? Should she not be interested in examining how her position has been affected by the changing processes in the socio-economic life of modern Africa? It is her duty to critically evaluate her position in her society and give her reactions to issues which concern her. Doing so does not make her anti-society, rather, ignoring it portrays her as naive, unintelligent and incapable of determining what is good for herself.

According to most literary theorists, feminism is politics, which aims to change the status of women in the society:

> Feminism is a politics directed at changing existing power relations between women and men in society. These power relations structure all areas of life, the family, education and welfare, the worlds of work and politics, culture and leisure. They determine who does what and for whom, what we are and what we might become.[3]

The fact that a body of politics – feminism – aims at changing existing chains of relationships between men and women in the society indicates that such relationships are problematic. Why then should anybody feel apologetic for contributing towards the rectification of a problematic situation, especially when this whole affair concerns his or her well-being? Why then should African women shy away or refrain from any utterance that might suggest that they are feminists? And why should men so strongly detest women who display any feminist leanings? This position gives the impression that there is something wrong with being a feminist. At this point, one may like to ask the following questions: should being a feminist impair the woman's prospects of finding a husband; does being a feminist in any way imply inadequacy in a wife or mother; does it indicate inability to carry out the woman's duties in the home effectively? The answer of course is an emphatic 'no'.

It is therefore amazing that our intellectuals, especially women writers among them, seem apologetic to admit that they are feminists, even when their writings constitute clear indications of their feminist inclinations. Such denial as Ogundipe-Leslie rightly puts it is a result of

> ... the successful intimidation of African women by men over the issues of women's liberation and feminism. Male ridicule, aggression and backlash have resulted in making women apologetic and have given the term feminist, a bad name.[4]

It is perhaps this 'successful intimidation' of women by men buttressed by the perpetuation of grossly inadequate and conservative tradition that prompted writers like Buchi Emecheta and Flora Nwapa to state that they are not feminists. 'Yet nothing can be more feminist than the writings of these women writers in their concern for and deep understanding of experiences and fates of women in the society'.[5]

Such denial gives an impression that both the African woman and the man lack a thorough understanding of the main objectives of feminism especially the African brand of it. This paper which aims principally at highlighting the feminist inclinations of Flora Nwapa starts by pinpointing the underlying ideology and the focus of this relatively new approach to the analysis of several relationships in society as they concern the woman. In the first place,

> A genuine African feminism recognizes a common struggle with African men for the removal of the yokes of foreign domination and European/American exploitation. It is not antagonistic to men but challenges them to be aware of certain salient aspects of women's subjugation which differ from the generalized oppression of all African peoples.[6]

Thus it aims at highlighting the inequities in the male/female relationship in our society, with a view to changing institutionalised subjugation, intimidation and oppression of women. African feminism or more precisely a feminist approach to our social life, our literature, provides the opportunity of re-evaluating attitudes and misconceptions about women, which have been buttressed all along both by African culture and the misogynous traditions of the European colonial masters. Certainly, since the aims and objectives of African feminism do not hamper the woman's operation as a wife or mother, but rather seeks to bring about the establishment of more equitable conditions, better understanding and a more cordial relationship between man and woman, it is an ideology that should be supported by all, especially the women. As de Beauvoir posits,

> It is for man to establish the reign of liberty in the midst of the world of the given. To gain supreme victory, it is necessary, for one thing, that by and through their natural differentiation, men and women unequivocally affirm their brotherhood.[7]

If de Beauvoir's objectives should be achieved, then our intellectual male and female alike, should feel neither threatened nor embarrassed by the development of feminist critical perspectives both in our literature and in other facets of our social life.

Having stated rather briefly the main focus of feminism generally, and that of the African brand in particular, the paper will now proceed with the examination of works by Flora Nwapa while underscoring the feminist perspectives of her writing.

Although Nwapa has written on various themes including the Nigerian civil war, she has most often made the experiences of the African woman in relation to those themes the central concern of her creative works. In her three novels, *Efuru*, *Idu* and *One is Enough*,[8] the author focuses on family life, a rather broad theme which allows her to explore the life of the African woman within her society. She discusses the woman's reactions to several issues which affect her as a woman and as a member of a specific cultural group; her interactions and role within her society; her perception of self as well as the society's perception of her.

In *Efuru* her first novel, focusing her narrative on Efuru the beautiful daughter of Nwashike Ogene; Adizua her husband a nonentity; Ajanupu, her mother-in-law's sister; Eneberi her second husband, and a network of friends and relations, the author explores family life in her own part of Igbo land. Discussing her people's life – their joys and tribulations, occupations and various activities – Nwapa draws attention to the position of the woman in the realm of things; her dreams, fulfilled and unfulfilled.

In the worlds of Nwapa's three books and in Igbo world-view generally, a grown up woman earns the respect of her people if she is married. She becomes fully integrated into her husband's family if she bears children. But she becomes entitled to any material inheritance only through her male children. In view of all this, the heroines of Nwapa's three books are fated to spend several sleepless nights, as they find themselves wanting in

various degrees and at various points in time. The author pain-
stakingly depicts the predicament of a childless woman represented by Efuru and Idu, heroines of her first two novels, and
Amaka in her third novel *One is Enough*. This she does in a manner
indicative of her deep concern for the suffering of such women.

Through gossip and conversations, reminiscent of women,
Nwapa reverberates the problems of women generally and of the
childless women in particular. As is characteristic of village life,
everyone has the right to express an opinion on any issue whether
or not it concerns them. Thus

> Efuru's neighbours talked as they were bound to talk. They did not
> see the reason why Adizua should not marry another woman since,
> according to them, two men do not live together. To them Efuru was
> a man since she could not produce.[9]

A woman who is unable to bear children is a 'failure', a man
rather than a woman. One is not surprised then that

> Efuru was very worried in the second year of her marriage. 'My
> mother had only me' she said one night to herself. 'My father told me
> so and also that she found it difficult to become pregnant. Am I going
> to be like my mother? But if I am going to be like her, then I too will
> have a daughter like her. But what if that is denied me? What will
> I do? oh, what will I do? she wept. Efuru did not sleep that night.[10]

Efuru's lamentation is full of anguish; the anguish and despera-
tion of an unfulfilled individual who feels her selfworth has
become drastically reduced because she has failed to perform
that function which determines her value to her community. She
must face humiliation and denigration; the fate reserved for a
childless woman in the traditional African society and even in the
Africa of more modern setting.

However, Nwapa's feminist approach to the portraiture of
her heroine has rescued the doomed Efuru. Rather than condemn
or abandon her to frustration, Nwapa shows that the woman
deserves credit for a great deal of other things than procreation
alone. She also indicates that a woman should as of necessity
take part in making decisions about issues which affect her. First
of all, Efuru is introduced to the reader as a beautiful woman
of honourable descent, the daughter of the well-known and

respected Nwashike Ogene – 'mighty man of valour'. But Efuru elopes and marries Adizua, an inconsequential nonentity, who cannot afford to pay the traditional bride-price, because he was her own choice.

A conservative non-feminist view would see Efuru as an obstinate child, who brings shame and humiliation to her father. But from a feminist perspective, she is a strong-willed, rebellious young woman, who respects and observes the traditions of her people, but who, at the same time rejects those aspects which seek to oppress and dwarf her personality. For instance, she accepts the traditional 'bath' but firmly rejects the idea of an arranged marriage; nor would she succumb to long years of living apart from the man she loves while he works and saves money for the bride-price. Rather she runs away and lives with him and together they work to save the substantial amount required.

By marrying Adizua, she shatters the expectations of her society. When she finds that farm work does not suit her she is equally decisive: 'I am not cut out for farm work. I am going to trade' (p. 10).

She is a responsible and determined woman who orders her priorities appropriately. The same is true of most other female characters in Flora Nwapa's fiction. The author however realises the danger of alienation and has therefore created for her heroines opportunities of self-fulfilment which will not distance them from the society, from the people. She also recognises the necessity for people to view themselves as free members of their society. Such frame of mind facilitates a most conducive atmosphere for the growth of an analytical mind. It encourages the individual to reject questionable norms or oppressive policies, rather than accept them simply because the society prescribes them.

For as John Harris rightly puts it:

> We must remember that to deny someone control of their own lives is to offer them a most profound insult, not to mention the injury which the frustration of their wishes and the setting at naught of their own plans for themselves will add.[11]

In concurrence with Harris' opinion above, Flora Nwapa creates in Efuru a character who takes control of her life, who creates a unique image for herself. Rather than place Efuru on the periphery of activities Flora Nwapa allots a decisive role to her. Efuru thus becomes a cynosure, the centre without which all other things fall apart. By juxtaposing the character of Efuru with that of Adizua, the author creates an admirable personality, respectful daughter, resourceful woman, dutiful wife and, in the end, mother. Viewed against the character of Adizua, an unsuccessful farmer who lacks even the guts to tell his wife that he is fond of her and wishes to stay close to her (p. 20), a flirt and an irresponsible husband and father, Efuru's personality towers over and dwarfs the image of Adizua – a caricature of a man.

In this same way, she excels, when compared with her second husband Eneberi. She is industrious, considerate, has a high moral standard and shows high regard for the reasonable norms of her society, while Eneberi is an egocentric liar and a thief. Nevertheless, Efuru knows when to stop and think. By turning her back eventually on marriage and dedicating herself to the services of the lake goddess, Flora Nwapa's heroine negates and thwarts certain Igbo concepts about the woman, especially that embodied in: 'Di bu mma ogori' (p. 97) or 'Ugwu nwanyi bu di' ('A husband is a woman's beauty and respect'). Efuru confirms Flora Nwapa's own contention as well as the opinion of her mother-in-law that:

> The route to (women's) liberation is economic power ... all women married or single must be economically independent. 'If it means selling oranges, then we sell oranges' to be financially autonomous.[12]

Having achieved economic independence, Efuru is able to give up marriage, once her two husbands fail to live up to her expectations. Back in her father's house she takes charge of all affairs and discharges both her civic and other responsibilities honourably. These include the provision of medical treatment for some members of the community who may otherwise have suffered and died neglected.

Thus, by alloting principal roles to her heroines (which are not necessarily connected with marriage), Ms Nwapa creates female characters who have achieved a stature usually only associated with men in the Igbo communities of *Efuru*. Thanking Efuru, the daughter of Nnona, one of her benefactors said:

> ... I want to say again that we are happy that you have helped our mother. You have done what only men are capable of doing and so you have done like a man.[13]

Thus the author has brought a feminist angle into her narrative; an approach which implicitly condemns the peripheralisation of women in the realm of affairs.

In *Idu* as in *Efuru*, Ms Nwapa depicts family life. This time activities rotate around Idu, who is also initially childless. Like Efuru, Idu as a character dwarfs and over-shadows other characters around her, male or female. She is industrious, hardworking and a loving wife.

Obviously, Ms Nwapa's women characters are hardly 'cut out for farm-work'. For Idu has also displayed a commendable business acumen, which even her husband and her gossiping neighbours recognise with great admiration. Idu is an amiable person and in spite of some petty jealousy among women, she is a woman 'pleasing not only to her husband' but one loved and respected by almost everybody.

Writing from a feminist perspective, Flora Nwapa continues to raise issues which are problematic to family life generally, and particularly to the woman who acts as a touchstone in the family. For a great deal of the man's joy as a married man and full-fledged member of his society depends on the woman.

In her treatment of unfulfilled marriage in *Efuru*, the author indicates the agony which is generated in Efuru's life by her secondary infertility, by the high rate of infant mortality, as well as the irresponsibility of the men she has associated with. In presenting another unfulfilled marriage in *Idu* the author juxtaposes two childless families, (at least at the initial stages of their growth) and through this device she indicates that the woman is not always responsible for childlessness in marriage, while through conversation between two friends – Idu and Ojiugo – she also shows how unhappy this problem has made the two women. Using as sub-plots stories about minor characters, Ms Nwapa imbues her major characters with hopes of a fulfilled future and confidence in themselves. Typical of such situations are stories about Nwakuma, Anedi, and Onyeazo – women who were once prostitutes. From their immoral lifestyles of prostitution, a lifestyle which is unacceptable both to the community and to the goddess of the lake, these women have settled down to normal family life and have been blessed with children.

Flora Nwapa indicates that all humans, male or female, under normal conditions are capable of progressive development, often as a result of self-examination. To consolidate this argument, she incorporates vivid flashbacks, which give her readers insights on the past lives of some of her characters. Their radical change from reckless irresponsible and immoral lives to those of responsible and respected members of their society is a sign of their growth. It is this kind of natural evolution, inspired from the inside, voluntary rather than imposed or used as an oppressive measure against any group as a sex, that has been effectively employed as an implement for characterisation. This approach has inspired a self-purification motivated by spiritual growth rather than the type of self-preservation in which some female characters in African literature are often involved. The self-restraint often illogical and involuntary, shown by such women is merely to ensure their marriageability. In other words they preserve themselves for the man. Typical examples of such characters are in Grace Ogot's 'The Old White Witch'. Here, female characters gave up their financial assets in order to ensure that they find husbands. Such characters create an impression of self-worthlessness, a situation they now strive to rectify through marriage.

To remedy her women characters from moral degradation and degeneration, Ms Nwapa introduces some cultural constraints in the image of the goddess Uhamiri, popularly known by her worshippers as 'our mother', revered by women and men alike. The desire to please the goddess has brought many wayward women back home, entirely changed, settled and effectively fulfilling their functions as the centre, the live-wire of their families. For Uhamiri does not only forgive women who have shown remorse for their inadequacies, but as encouragement to persist, she has also rewarded them with fertility.

In the image of the goddess Uhamiri, Ms Nwapa has thus created a feminine symbol of chastity, a chastity which evolves as an indication of the natural growth of her heroines, rather than one enforced by chauvinist prescriptions. This movement towards a non-enforced self-purification accounts for the painful desertion of Amarajeme by Ojiugo. It would have been easy for Ojiugo to continue to live with her husband Amarajeme and pretend that her unborn baby belongs to him. More so because that would have implied Amarajeme's capability to father a child. He would have been spared the humiliation emanating from that notion of 'not being a man', the most shameful attribute to any man in his society. It is the revelation of this shortcoming in him that led him to commit suicide. However, Flora Nwapa's heroine would not conform with such an arrangement, because this would put her in a situation of self-defilement and adultery. In other words, Nwapa, like overt feminists is saying that if a men is allowed the freedom to choose his lifestyle then the woman should also be allowed a similar freedom. Anything less would imply the intellectual inferiority of the woman.

Some critics have dismissed Ms Nwapa as a non-serious writer who fills the pages of her books with 'unnecessary detailed descriptions and conversations by a galaxy of women'. Such critics have dismissed the day to day concerns and activities of women as unimportant and therefore not worth describing. Jean Grimshaw succinctly describes the situation thus:

> This implicitly derogatory attitude to women is linked both to an over-monolithic account of male power and to a failure to give much attention to the ways in which women have, in fact, often spent much of their lives, and to activities which have been particularly theirs (such as the rearing of children, for example).[14]

Fortunately however, some women are waking up though rather late to their responsibility to their own sex generally and to themselves as individuals by making the activities of women the central theme of their literary works. Ms Nwapa's novels and almost all her short stories put her among the foremost of these. In simple but clear language, often employing that special brand of English identifiable with writers from West Africa, Ms Nwapa recreates the life she knows best – the life of women. She portrays her women realistically as normal human beings with all their imperfections, yet imbued with a great deal of virtue and admirable sense of responsibility. The author does not set out to idealise her heroines, but illuminates the best in them as she criticises their negative qualities. But most importantly, her works indicate that the woman, her activities, her wishes fulfilled and otherwise, joys and tribulations are all worthy themes for discussion in our fiction.

In her fourth novel, *One is Enough*, the author investigates another situation in the life of a childless woman. At a first reading the three novels, *Efuru*, *Idu* and *One is Enough*, might

seem merely to be describing family life in Igbo land, particularly, the riverine Igbo tribe to which the author herself belongs.
But a deeper study of the three books shows that in each the
author investigates various complexities relating to life. She
demonstrates as she does so, the reactions of and to the heroines
at the centre of the narratives. In the first two, activities are
all set in the village, while the scene in *One is Enough* starts
off in a semi-urban area and ends up in Nigeria's capital city,
Lagos.

In this last book, Ms Nwapa's depiction of the relationship
between Amaka and her mother-in-law evokes the usual stereo-
typical mother and daughter-in-law relationship. The image of the
mother-in-law is of a nagging scold who lacks a proper understanding of her daughter-in-law's predicament. Through this image,
which contrasts sharply with that of Efuru's mother-in-law in
Efuru, Nwapa stresses the need for solidarity among women, so
relevant to all feminists and women's liberation movements. This
solidarity, however, cannot flourish without a good understanding on the part of women themselves that all women – mothers,
mothers-in-law, daughters, or daughters-in-law are all second
class citizens. True it is that Amaka herself in a conversation with
a newly married woman (who has just narrated how she was
beaten up by her husband) commented on the behaviour of
African men thus:

> ... The trouble with our men is their ego. They refuse to appreciate
> their wives. Mind you, they do appreciate their mothers and sisters,
> but never their wives.[15]

The truth is, however, that no woman is free from the effect of
this lack of appreciation by the menfolk or bluntly put, of being
treated by the society as a nonentity. For a mother was once a
wife, subjugated by her husband while a sister who soon becomes
a wife automatically becomes her husband's slave. No woman
irrespective of class is free from male dominance.

Some feminist theorists have asked the question: are women
oppressed first as women or in their roles in society, as means of
production? The African woman suffers oppression in both roles
whether she is an aristocrat or not. She is the society's under-
dog, seen and not heard, obedient to the husband, her master
and her lord. To save themselves from this male oppression and

dominance therefore, women must realise the need for solidarity and sisterhood. But Ms Nwapa's depiction of some mother/daughter-in-law relationships show them to be lacking in this realisation. Below is an excerpt from a verbal encounter between Amaka and her mother-in-law:

> Amaka: Mother forgive me. It will not happen again. I should not have replied to what you said, I am very sorry, mother. Please, don't throw me away, mother.[16]

This apology should have mollified even the most hard-hearted person especially when the offence was quite trivial. But the older lady's response is hostile and uncompromising:

> Mother-in-law: The hold you have on my son will end today . . . I have waited for six years, and I cannot wait for even one day more . . . Tell me, you said I knew your plight. What is your plight? You are barren. That's all, barren. A year or so ago, you said you had a miscarriage. My son came to tell me. I laughed at him. I did not let him know that you were deceiving him. So, my son's wife, you were never pregnant and you never will be. Get that clear in your mind.[17]

The bitterness and insensitivity displayed by the older lady, the product of self-centredness, will never nurture the much-needed sisterhood. Ms Nwapa is thus through differing relationships between women re-echoing the feminist contention of the absolute necessity for cordial relationships among women.

One is Enough is dedicated to her mother-in-law whom she says attaches a great deal of importance to the economic independence of women, be they married or single. This concept is one of the underlying ideological concepts of African feminism, especially as stressed by Philomina Chioma Steady.

Ms Nwapa's heroines demonstrate her own agreement with feminists in this respect. All her heroines, Efuru, Idu and Amaka, display this striving for economic independence. The portrayals climax in Amaka who does not only earn enough money to buy herself a car, buy herself a plot of land on which she builds a personal house, but also to buy her own freedom by returning the bride-price to her ex-husband.

Ms Nwapa has devoted three novels to women and women centred activities. She has given prominence to the discussion of the said activities in a way that indicates strongly shared ideological concepts with feminists. Most importantly, she has created characters whose quest for self-fulfillment does not alienate them from their social milieu, but rather strengthens their position in the society. It is in recognition of her achievement in connection with the presentation of the woman and the explication of women related issues, most often from a feminist perspective that one may conveniently regard her as a feminist.

NOTES

1. According to A. Eldhom, Harris and Young, who distinguished three aspects of reproduction, the reproduction of the labour force refers to the process by which the products of procreation become workers: e.g. schooling, imparting to them the skills necessary to participate in the agricultural process.
2. Molara Ogundipe-Leslie, 'African Women, Culture and Another Development', *Journal of African Marxists*, 5 (February, 1984/89) 35-6.
3. C. Weedon, *Feminist Practice and Poststructuralist Theory* (New York: Basil Blackwell Inc., 1987) 1.
4. Ogundipe-Leslie 'African Women, Culture and Another Development', 11.
5. 'African Women', 11.
6. Philomina Chioma Steady, *African Woman Cross-Culturally* (Cambridge: Cambridge University Press, 1981).
7. Simone de Beauvoir, *The Second Sex*, trans. and ed. H. M. Parshley (1953). Reprint (New York: Vintage Books, 1974).
8. Flora Nwapa, *Efuru* (London: Heinemann Educational Books, 1966). Flora Nwapa, *Idu* (London: Heinemann Educational Books, 1970). Flora Nwapa, *One is Enough* (Enugu: Tana Press, 1981).
9. Nwapa, *Efuru*, 24.
10. Nwapa, *Efuru*, 24.
11. John Harris, 'Political Status of Children', in *Contemporary Political Philosophy*, ed. Keith Graham (Cambridge: Cambridge University Press, 1982) 35-55.
12. Interview with Katherine Frank, Freetown, Sierra Leone, 1983.
13. Nwapa, *Efuru*, 132.
14. Jean Grimshaw, 'Autonomy and Identity in Feminist Thinking' in *Feminist Perspectives in Philosophy*, eds Morevena Griffiths and Margaret Whitford (Bloomington and Indianapolis: Indiana University Press, 1988).
15. Nwapa, *One is Enough*, 30.
16. Nwapa, *One is Enough*, 3.
17. Nwapa, *One is Enough*, 15, 16.

Index